BACK ON THE RAILS

BACK ON THE RAILS

A Journey Through Career Transition

AJ Clinkenbeard

Back on the Rails

A Journey Through Career Transition

Copyright © 2019 Adam J Clinkenbeard

www.brightsideadvisers.com

First Printing – July 2019

All rights reserved. No part of this book may be reproduced or transmitted in any form or by any means whatsoever without express written permission from the author, except in the case of brief quotations embodied in critical articles and reviews.

ISBN: 9781079158755

Dedication

This book is dedicated to my loving and supportive wife, Angela. Your resolute belief in me, that I can do anything, guided me through career transition and motivated me to write this book. I'm grateful for the patience and encouragement you showed while I was feverishly networking to find my next career home. The love we share fuels me every day to be the best husband, friend, father, and giver I can be. Thank you, soulmate!

Acknowledgments

I'd like to thank Lynee Miller, Shelly Eddy, Bill Waham, James Laidlaw, Randy Butler, and Chris Spanier. You are good friends, and I appreciate the support and camaraderie we shared.

Thanks to Natalie Ruppert, Brian Holbrook, Bill Carigan, Marcie Taylor, Steve Browne and Pat Frew for creating formal networking groups that support professionals in career transition.

Thanks to Todd Pfister, Dave Gooch, Preston Bowles, Paul Miklautsch, and Garth Geist for instilling a new sense of confidence in me.

And I appreciate the hundreds of other people who graciously invested their time to network with me. You not only made more connections, but you also urged me on to victory.

A huge thank you goes out to Tom Anderle for walking me through the most thorough career-pathing exercise of my life. You helped me set my course, and I'm forever grateful...I'll be sure to pay it forward.

A heartfelt thank you goes out to Bob Tubesing. "Writers write!" he said. So, I started writing. Thanks for the swift kick in the behind!

Special Thanks

My best friend, Justin King, told me to share my story just a few days after I lost my job. I told him he was out of his mind. Three months later, I called and told him I would write it, and I asked that he be my accountability partner. Mission accomplished!

Abby, thanks for being my cheerleader every day!

Finally, thank you Mom and Dad. You gave me what I needed all along the way. Perfect doses at perfect intervals.

Table of Contents

1 - Parting 1
2 – Pondering 11
3 – Present 23
4 – Plugged In.. 33
5 – Pointed & Purposeful 47
6 – Process-oriented 69
7 – Performance & Pride 79
8 – Prospecting 89
9 – Perseverance & Pride..................................... 101
10 – Peer Support 113
11 – Prepared & Practice 125
12 – Payday 133
Summary 141
About the Author 149

1 - Parting

The traffic on the way to the office was unusually light, perhaps because it was the day after Labor Day. Construction frequently added fifteen extra minutes to Ken's commute, but he sailed down the highway this morning. The long weekend brought some needed rest and relaxation. Ken had been working long days over the last six weeks to finish an important project. His team selflessly put in overtime each period, ensuring everything met the highest of standards.

Ken slowly pulled into the parking lot, enjoying the last bit of 90's rock playing on his radio. A smile came across his face – he loved his job. He considered himself blessed to come to work each day at a place where he makes a difference in the lives of others. Parkwood Safety Equipment manufactured several lines of safety gear for law enforcement, first responders, search and rescue teams and fire departments. Ken's team created instructional material and compiled user manuals to ensure the equipment was used properly.

An important new line of equipment had just entered the final stages of testing and was about to get the green light for production. Ken's team was tasked to deliver the instruction manuals before Labor Day so that Parkwood's president, Mike, could update the investors with the good news that they were ahead of schedule. The investors needed good news, as Parkwood failed to finalize two strategic acquisitions earlier in the year, putting the company far behind their revenue targets.

Satisfied that he'd met his goal, Ken confidently walked into the office and down the hallway to his cubicle. He was the first one there, as usual. And he couldn't wait for his team to arrive so they could celebrate achieving their goal.

Ken opened his email and began organizing his day. The morning would serve as his catch-up time since he'd pushed several other projects aside to finish the manuals. After lunch, he had two conference calls and one meeting. With gaps in his calendar, Ken planned to use this day as the springboard for starting on his upcoming projects.

Once the team finally arrived, Ken gathered them around for a quick huddle.

"First, I want to thank all of you from the bottom of my heart for all of the great work you did to create the instruction manuals. These were our best yet and required very few revisions. Great job! And thank you for all the long hours you put in so that we could hit our deadline. The effort didn't go unnoticed. John emailed me over the weekend and congratulated the team. Mike is meeting with investors today, and he'll share that our efforts helped the project go into production by the end of the month. Again, thank you!" Ken said.

"Wow!" exclaimed Anita, "I'm so happy that everything turned out okay. I was nervous last week and thought we'd have more to touch up today."

"No, we really nailed it this time. Everyone came together, and we held each other accountable for excellence. We're a force to be reckoned with," said April.

"I agree," Ken concurred. "This team performed at its peak. And I know we can replicate that success on our next project. Let's meet up this afternoon at 3pm to review the next project and set up our timeline."

The group high-fived and continued complimenting each other on a job well-done. Moments later, they disbursed to their cubicles to start the day.

Ken sat down; a huge grin showed on his face. He thought to himself, "I'm so proud of this team. The sky's the limit. Nothing can stop us."

About an hour later, John, Ken's supervisor, called through the intercom.

"Ken, hey, do you have a few minutes to get together at 10 o'clock?" John asked.

Ken replied, "Yes, sir. I'll meet you in your office promptly at 10." The relationship between John and

Ken had always been more formal than most. But Ken always showed his superiors the utmost respect, perhaps a remnant of having a former Air Force Sergeant father. He was raised to say sir and ma'am.

"Great," John replied.

Ken looked at his watch. It was 9:40am. So, he quickly put together some talking points about the finished project and a summary plan for the projects on deck. He figured John would want to congratulate him and his team and hear about the department's plans. John was always asking about what was next.

A few minutes before 10:00am, Ken gathered his notes, a couple printouts, and his portfolio. He glided down the hallway, still on an emotional high from enjoying a win with his team. As he turned the corner into John's office, he saw Tia, the HR Director, sitting down across from John.

"Oh, I'm sorry. I didn't realize you were in a meeting," Ken apologized.

John started, "No, we were just waiting for you. Come on in and have a seat."

Instantly, Ken felt a pit in his stomach. He wondered why Tia would be there for a meeting with him. A million questions went through his mind, instantaneously. John got up from behind his desk, walked over to the door, and closed it. Ken's pulse quickened. He knew this wouldn't be good.

"Ken, I invited Tia in for this discussion," John started.

"Hey Ken," Tia said awkwardly.

"Hi, Tia. This certainly is a surprise. What's going on?" Ken inquired a bit sheepishly.

"Well Ken, as you know, things in your department haven't been going well for a while now. We really don't see you as a good fit in your role as Project Manager. So, we're going to let you go," John declared. He slowly slid a sheet of paper toward Ken. The heading read, Termination Statement.

Ken sat quietly, confused, and stunned. "What was John talking about? Things hadn't been going well? My team has hit each deadline on time or early. They'd delivered quality outputs. All our costs were in check. I just outlined our new department vision and discussed the details with John a few weeks ago. Where is this coming from?" Ken thought as he gazed around the room.

"Would you like to review this statement?" Tia asked.

Ken, still silent, looked at both Tia and John and then at the termination statement. He was still in disbelief. Ken bit his lower lip and began reading the brief reasoning for his forced departure. Only two justifications were listed.

- *Ken failed to produce a cohesive department vision*

- *Ken ignored important projects assigned to him and his team and missed key deadlines*

The first thing that went through Ken's mind was anger. Ken stared at the words. He read them again. They hadn't changed. "These were lies. What is happening?" he thought.

Ken took a deep breath. It took every fiber in his being not to erupt emotionally. He didn't even know which emotion might come out. Ken was a professional and could keep his emotions from getting the best of him. He took another deep breath and called upon all the diplomacy he had left. "John, I must be confused. I see here that you've listed two reasons for letting me go, but I'm certain that I've delivered a vision and we've met all our deadlines this year. What am I missing?"

"Ken, the fact is that you're not a fit here. The company isn't seeing this vision you speak of, and I've asked more than once that you focus on the prototype protection vests and ultra-lightweight fire helmets. But I don't have anything from you," John declared.

John threw a curveball. Ken couldn't even respond to the statement. They'd reviewed the vision with the entire executive team just two months prior. And John had only once mentioned the vests and helmets to his recollection. They agreed that those would be focus points in Q4, and they were both listed on the notes Ken had in hand. He did his best to reply. "Okay. I'm still confused. I don't recall us ever discussing how my lack of performance was leading down this path…"

John interrupted, "Ken. We did discuss your performance. Couple your struggles with our financial performance this year, and we had to make a decision that puts us ahead for the future. My decision is final. You don't have to sign the termination statement, but you can take a copy with you. Tia will walk you to your cubicle to gather your personal belongings. I wish you the best."

Ken, never the one to rock the boat, carefully picked up the paper from John's desk and looked at John for the last time. John's dark eyes bore no emotion, and his mouth made a slight smirk. Ken's face said it all. Pale and expressionless, it was the same look a disappointed parent gives a child. With a subtle head shake, Ken broke eye contact and walked out. Tia followed behind.

Ken's anger and surprise turned to shame. His head slumped while he paced back down the hall to his space, space he'd occupied for the last twelve years. Questions were flooding his mind. "Why is John lying? How did he get Mike to go along with this? How did he get Tia to go along with this? Why are they colluding against me? Where did this all go wrong? What do I tell my wife? What do I tell my kids? What do I tell my team? What do I tell my peers? How do I break this to my parents? What are my friends going to think? What am I going to do? How are my finances?" Before he knew it, he was walking into his department.

"Ken. Are you alright?" asked April as he walked past her desk.

At this point, he couldn't completely hide his emotions. And with Tia hot on his heels, he couldn't lie. "I'll be fine, April. Thanks for asking. Today's my last day here at Parkwood. Take care of the team for me."

April's mouth gaped open; her expression frozen. Her eyes widened. Only silence crossed her lips.

Not only did they fire Ken, but they convicted him to the walk of shame to collect his things. He'd overseen multi-million-dollar project budgets and managed expenses down to the penny. His integrity was beyond reproach. But now, as a former employee, he was being treated like a felon. Who knows what pens or post-its he might pilfer?

His desk was spartan. Apart from a few photos, Ken hadn't brought many items from home, and he had even fewer corporate mementos. He grabbed an empty box from the recycle bin under his desk and placed the few treasures inside.

Ken looked up at Tia and reached for his badge. "Here you go. I won't need this anymore," he said sheepishly.

"Thank you, Ken. I wish you the best," Tia replied.

"Do you need to walk me to the door?" Ken inquired.

"Unfortunately, yes," Tia responded, extending her hand.

Ken shook his head again in disbelief as he picked up his box and made his way to the door, Tia scurrying behind.

Less than two minutes after John dropped the bomb, Ken was out the employee-only back door and into the hallway. It was over. Twelve years of blood, sweat, and tears ended faster than the Kentucky Derby. All he could think about was how much he had given, how much he had sacrificed, how much he didn't deserve this disgraceful exit. Ken's bitterness grew with every footstep on the way to his car.

Ken settled in behind the wheel and turned the car on. He grabbed his phone and called his wife, Veronica. "Hey, sweetheart."

"What's wrong?" asked Veronica. The tone of Ken's voice indicated foul play. He was usually upbeat and positive, excited about life and work. But not today. She could hear a difference.

"I just got fired. John called me in his office and fired me. I have no idea where this came from," Ken said, his voice cracking at the end.

"I'm so sorry. We're going to be fine. You're going to be fine. We'll get through this," Veronica assured. "I have to get back to my class, so we'll talk about it tonight. You're awesome, and this is going to work out for the best. Don't worry. Go home and get some rest.

I love you." Veronica's ability to offer comfort when things went wrong was one of her strong suits.

Ken mumbled an I love you and hung up the phone. He sat there for a while, his mind still racing. Dozens of Parkwood memories created a highlight reel playing in his head. Birthdays, work anniversaries, meeting his wife, receiving promotions, employee of the year galas, traveling overseas, promoting teammates, and fun times with peers were just a few of the featured clips.

After another deep breath, he began his commute home, albeit much earlier than he'd anticipated. "At least there's no traffic right now," he thought.

Parkwood recollections continued to crowd Ken's mind until he got home. He felt like he was trapped in a dream. None of this seemed real. Ken held a job since he was fifteen and had never gone more than 3 months without working, and that was in his first year of college. For the last twenty-five years, he only knew life as a working professional. And now he wasn't working.

2 – Pondering

Wednesday morning broke the same as every other weekday. Ken was up early and went for a run. He took his daughter to school and went back home to make breakfast and prepare for the day. But today, he didn't iron a dress shirt or prepare his lunch. He sat at the breakfast bar and poured a cup of coffee, still in disbelief at the events from yesterday.

"What am I going to do?" he thought. He didn't even know where to start. Ken hadn't looked for a job in twelve years. He found Parkwood while working at another firm, absent the urgency and pressure mounting on him presently. He didn't know anything about the market, new job boards, LinkedIn, or networking. Ken felt like an analog player in a digital world.

The more he thought, the more his feelings, his negative feelings, built up. Ken was a disciplined man and prided himself for his emotional intelligence. He kept his emotions in check at work and avoided showing anger or sadness. Ken was consistent and reliable, the person that kept cool when things heated up. In fact, he seemed to thrive as pressure mounted, and he performed best when everything was on the line. His team and peers respected Ken's ability to deliver in the toughest of circumstances.

This was different. Ken was bruised and battered. His self-worth was in the toilet. Ken's identity was wrapped up in his role as a Senior Project Manager at Parkwood, and his star had been on the rise for the last half of his career there. A promotion to director looked to be on the near horizon, maybe a year away at most.

Yesterday's career setback produced a mental setback as well. Ken's cheerful and upbeat attitude was gone. He struggled to find things to smile about that morning, and he didn't want to go out in public. He still hadn't called his parents to break the news, and his brothers were in the dark too. It took everything he had just to tell his daughter, Abby, the night prior that her daddy didn't have a job. They both sobbed and held each other. Shame kicked confidence to the curb and took up residence.

Ken moped around the house most of the day. He watched bad daytime television and accomplished nothing. Most of the time, he found himself daydreaming, again playing reels of memories from good and not-so-good times at Parkwood. He thought about all the people he had helped and all the people that had helped him. By the afternoon, Ken's pity party was pitiful – he was the only one attending.

The phone rang. "Hello?" answered Ken.

"Hey, son! It's Dad. What's going on? I called your office, and they said you weren't in. Are you okay?" The jig was up. It was Ken's father, Jim.

"Oh, hey, Dad. Uh, yeah, I'm at home today," Ken offered awkwardly. But he wasn't fooling anyone.

"Really? I'm not buying it. You couldn't snow me back then, and you're not snowing me now. Talk to me," Jim encouraged.

"Dad, you know me too well. Here goes – I lost my job yesterday. And I was too embarrassed to call you." Ken suddenly felt lighter. He'd be dreading this conversation for over 24 hours. His dad had high expectations and was proud of his son's accomplishments. Letting him down was unthinkable. Ken, unsure how the rest of this conversation would play out, hadn't disappointed his old man since a brainless high school misstep almost thirty years ago. It was uncharted territory.

There was a brief silence on the line for about three seconds. It was long enough to allow the gravity of the situation set in. Jim was retired but served in the military after college and then worked almost thirty years as a high school principal. He was a disciplined man with a no-nonsense communication style. But this time he realized his son needed something different.

"Son. I'm very sorry to hear this news. The first thing you need to know is that your mom and I love you and we're here for you. I can't imagine what you're going through. Let's do this. Rather than try a conversation on the phone, would you mind if I came over? In say an hour?" Jim spent a lot of time helping people work through tragedies in his role as a principal. He'd consoled kids that had lost parents, siblings, and friends in acts of violence. Familiar with such circumstances, he knew to be a good listener and empathize.

"Sure," Ken agreed. "You're welcome to stay for dinner too if you'd like."

"Perfect. See you in an hour. I love you son."

Ken hung up the phone, partly relieved and partly anxious.

Sixty minutes went by in a blink. Jim rang the doorbell precisely one hour after hanging up the phone, his timeliness the byproduct of living bell-to-bell in a school.

"Come on in Dad," Ken said as he opened the door. Jim stopped halfway through the threshold and hugged Ken tight. Without any words, he strode through the hallway to the living room.

"Alright son; have a seat and let's talk. I know you've had a day to start processing this situation. What are you thinking? Where's your head at?" Jim asked. He clearly was wasting no time getting to the point.

"Well, I'm mad. And sad. And scared. Those are the three main emotions I'm feeling. Right now, I can't seem to shake my anger at John and Mike. They really blind-sided me with this. The termination statement was just a lie. How could they lie like that? And how could HR do nothing about it? I think everyone is just plain scared to question what they do. And then there was no class, no dignity to how they walked me out. It was like I was a criminal. Ugh! Those guys will get what they deserve. You know what they say about karma," Ken unloaded.

Jim didn't like what he was hearing, but he wanted Ken to get it all out. If the negativity stuck around, Ken wouldn't be able to move on and get himself prepared for the job search. Jim understood this was just the beginning. "Ok. I hear you. They surprised you with this firing, and it was fabricated and unfair. Is that right?" Jim clarified.

"Yes! I had been doing tons of work and delivering every project on time and under budget. Heck, I thought I was on the verge of another promotion. I just don't think they liked me." Ken continued, "I don't see how things could have been going any better. If they wanted more or something different, they certainly didn't tell me. I'm not a mind reader. I don't know why they didn't like me. Unreal! Those guys are real jerks. They don't care about anyone but themselves."

"So, things were going great? Just so I can get some context, what was so great?" Jim asked.

"We had just finished a major part of a project on time, and it was going to help us move a product into final testing. Our team was really working well; we were collaborating, and we were more efficient than in prior quarters. We were under budget for the year, and we were about to dig in on some projects that had been on the back burner. It felt like a year full of wins so far," Ken explained.

"From where you're sitting, the year was a success. I get it. How did it look from your boss's eyes? Did he see it the same? And tell me more about these other projects that were on hold." Jim could tell there was a disconnect from his son's perception and the reality that the executives at Parkwood were experiencing. If Jim could get Ken to identify that gap, they'd create a pathway for accepting the situation.

"I was under the impression John saw the same things. We didn't talk very much, which made me feel like I was doing everything right. I figured he was the type of boss that only got involved when things went wrong. So, my team and I; we did our thing. Not a lot of oversight. It was the same with the other projects. John asked once about them, and I let him know they were in the queue," answered Ken.

They recounted details and replayed conversations for another hour. With his son's perspective outlined, Jim decided to challenge Ken to change perspectives. "Son, I think you could have missed something. Your boss's disinterest may have been a warning sign," Jim countered.

Ken became defensive. "Come on, Dad. He was just busy dealing with a couple other underperforming departments. He let the marketing VP go a few months ago, and he still hasn't replaced the Director of Client Success. John is up to his elbows in added duties. We were the last thing he'd be worried about."

"Good working relationships are key to long-term success. No offense son, but it doesn't sound like you and John were close. What did you do to build the relationship?" Jim countered. He already knew the answer.

"Hmm…I guess I'd say we weren't close. He wasn't like other supervisors I've had. He really never made any attempt to get to know me. I just assumed he was an introvert or just didn't care to know his employees. You taught me to build my half of every relationship. But I didn't get very far with John," Ken recalled.

Jim sat silent, letting those last thoughts sink in. Ken's reality still hadn't caught up with the real reality. Jim needed Ken to keep thinking through what had happened and to get his emotions under control. Without accepting the situation and by choosing to ignore the other side of the story, Ken would fail to get closure. Closure would be key to pursuing a new job.

Jim started, "I know this situation is still new to you, and you're wrestling with several emotions. You're angry, resentful, hurt, confused, and embarrassed. This is normal. In fact, I'd be worried if you didn't feel this way. May I give you some fatherly advice?"

"Of course, Dad," Ken replied.

"Take the next few days and process this entire situation. You need to ponder, get reflective, and open your mind. Don't go out looking for jobs, don't apply on job boards, and don't make a mess on social media. Just think through this. Most importantly, let your emotions flow. You'll probably feel a little like you're on a roller coaster, but that's expected. This may sound strange, but you need to grieve first. It's okay to be sad, disappointed, and melancholy." Jim's vast experience with people and emotions allowed him to succinctly deliver counsel to his son.

Jim continued, "Most people don't know what closure feels like. They think that a few magic words will do the trick. Closure happens when you accept full accountability for your circumstances. It's when you can no longer blame anyone else for what you're facing. And you can't fool yourself into believing it. Otherwise, everyone else will see and feel your fake attitude. I encourage you to be prayerful or keep a journal or enter a meditation regimen or see a counselor. The sooner you work through your emotions and get closure, the sooner you can move toward the next chapter in your career."

"Okay, Dad. I'll think this through. And I'll take your advice. Maybe we can get together at the end of the week and talk some more," Ken suggested.

"I'd like that very much, son," Jim replied. They spent the next several minutes chatting about Veronica and the kids. Ken promised to call his dad at the end of the week for a second meeting.

For the next three days, Ken wrestled with his emotions. The first day he was filled with anger and resentment. The entire situation and how it went down was unfair. He considered contacting an attorney and suing for wrongful termination. He called his best friends and vented. Ken found himself frequently damning Mike and John under his breath. He wanted them to fail. He wanted karma to swoop in and deal them bad hands, to torpedo their careers and ruin them financially.

But Ken's conscience, the little angel on his shoulder, kept reminding him that such negative thoughts were unproductive and unnecessary. Ken thought, "What am I thinking? I'm not a person who wishes ill-will on others. This type of thinking is not going to produce anything useful. I really don't want them to fail. If Mike and John fail, all my friends and colleagues will fail too."

By that evening, his anger turned to grief. He holed up in the ground floor rec room and asked not to be disturbed. Veronica obliged. She could tell Ken needed some alone time. Ken felt like a failure; like all of his worth had vanished. He was just plain sad. He missed his work, his team, his friends in other departments and his value. Tears began to well up in his eyes, and the good cry he needed finally hit.

The next morning brought another emotion in the series his dad foretold. Confusion. Ken's mind swirled as he retraced weeks and months of events searching for the genesis of the sequence that led to his dismissal. Could it have been when he didn't remind John about being out of town for a conference? Or maybe when they arrived separately at a client meeting, neither one knowing the other would be there? Perhaps the three-week period where they had no correspondence was the tipping point. Ken racked his brain, trying to figure out exactly how it all transpired. He was consumed by this obsession all day.

Ken didn't get much sleep that night, his mind whirling until the wee hours.

Daybreak introduced another emotion, anxiety. Ken had never been a nervous man, but he felt stricken by a fear of the unknown. He worried about finances most of all. How would he afford basic needs and medical insurance? Could he still pay for his daughter to go to college next year? What could they sell for extra cash? How much would unemployment pay? A countless stream of questions without answers.

When his reminder alarm went off at 2:30pm to pick up Abby from school, Ken realized he forgot to eat lunch. His anxiety was off the charts. He turned on some of his favorite 90's music in the car on his commute to the high school. It calmed him down. When Abby got in the car, they had a lively discussion about her day and the drama of her junior year. The rest of the evening, he focused on his family, avoiding the self-imposed inquisition from earlier.

Before Ken went to bed, he caught the ending scene from the movie *Back to the Future*. In it, George McFly says to his son, "If you put your mind to it, you can accomplish anything." The word, accomplish, stood out. Ken had always been an achiever, a goal-setter, someone that chased down results. But in the last few days, he couldn't tally one win, one accomplishment. He could accept defeat, or he could rally and put his mind to it. And his mind went to it, keeping him awake with dreams and goals galore.

Ken woke up on Friday with a mission. He needed wins today. Before breakfast, he made a list of chores and errands. He mapped out a plan to complete them, and he got to it. As he crossed off items from the list, he began to feel better. His confidence surged through the day. He began to feel like his old self, a winner, a guy who got things done. Ken dialed the phone: time to tell dad.

"Dad. I'm ready to talk again. Can I come by your place tomorrow morning?" Ken asked.

"Sure thing, son. I'll have the coffee on. See you then!" Jim said excitedly.

3 – Present

Before Ken's finger could press the doorbell, Jim opened the front door and shouted, "Good morning, son! It's great to see you!"

"Wow, Dad! What a reception! You always know how to make me feel welcome," Ken said with a smile.

"Get in here and let's settle into some dark roast. I just poured your cup," Jim said as he reached for the two mugs on the counter. "Let's go into the den." Ken followed his dad through the kitchen and into the hallway that led to the den. "Your mom is at yoga this morning, but she said hi."

"Tell her I said hi. I'll have to call her this afternoon," Ken offered. They entered the brightly lit den, the sun shining brightly between the open blinds. Ken's dad admired how the natural light created a welcoming glow that contrasted the dark wooden bookcases and furniture. The environment calmed and uplifted the weary and troubled souls that sought Jim's counsel on many occasions.

As they sat down, Jim opened, "Alright. It's been a few days since we talked. You sounded like there was a breakthrough. Fill me in."

"Well, Dad, first, you were right." They both laughed. It's rare for a son to admit his father is right. "I went through a lot of emotions. It was very uncomfortable. You know I've been proud of how I manage my emotions. Like you, I like to believe my emotional quotient is quite high. But it was low for the last three days. I went from anger to resentment to grief to anxiety. And there were probably some others in between. But last night it really hit me like a ton of bricks – I'm the same person today that I was on Tuesday morning. The only difference is my job title. I'm a winner, and I'm ready to go win again." Ken's smile and posture verified his words.

"I'm impressed with what you're telling me. What triggered the sudden change?" Jim probed.

"I was in a pretty low place most of the day yesterday. Late last night I was watching some television, and a random quote hit me. And I got to thinking about a lot of other insights I'd gained and shared through the years. I can only control my actions and reactions. I realized that I could either stay defeated or I could start acting like a winner again," Ken shared as he took a sip of his coffee.

"Sounds simple; maybe too good to be true," Jim doubted.

"You're right. Am I cured and 100% over this episode? No. But I'm miles ahead of where I was. I have to get into the present, and my present is unemployment. My present doesn't include Parkwood. It's not natural to say that yet," Ken admitted. He hadn't said the word unemployment out loud. It lingered in his mind, and he suddenly realized that accepting his new circumstance, getting into the present, would be a process. Today was the beginning of that journey.

Jim recognized the disappointed look on his son's face. The last time he saw it was when Ken missed out on a job promotion in his early days at Parkwood. Ken thought he was further along and now faced the grim reality that he had a long way to go.

"Son, emotions are fickle," Jim started. "The moment you think you've conquered them, they surprise you. It's going to take a few weeks to fully accept what happened and where you are now. And your emotions will rear their ugly heads in waves. I'm telling you this so you can be prepared for what's to come."

"You mean I'm not close to closure?" Ken asked meekly, grabbing his temples and rubbing.

"You're closer than I thought you'd be. You're in tune with your feelings, and you've verbalized your situation. But saying it once isn't enough. You're going to have to say "I lost my job" a lot. Owning your situation means telling yourself and telling others. Am

I making sense?" Jim wanted to be sure that Ken was still with him.

"Yes. I get it. Dad, I lost my job!" Ken exclaimed. Jim, a bit startled, laughed, and almost spilled his coffee. "I'll start by telling the family. I'm sure I can let them all know by tomorrow night. And I'll tell my close friends. I haven't talked to Justin or Stacy for a while, and they need to know. Plus, I know they'll support me."

Jim agreed, "They sure will. You'll be surprised how much support you'll get, and from some unlikely sources."

"This has been a great talk. In some ways, I'm looking forward to sharing my story. I can't lie, I'm a little nervous too," Ken admitted.

"That's to be expected, son. Before you leave, I want to make one more point. The hardest part of this journey will be the first step, the one where you accept what happened and take accountability for the part you played. It's the only path to closure. You won't be able to get back into the workforce until you get comfortable with your present," Jim waxed. "Any resentment or anger or bitterness you keep will unveil itself. It will show up when you meet new people. It will sabotage you in the interview process with prospective employers. Such conduct will certainly doom you, and you cannot allow that to happen."

"Dad, I may sound naive in saying this, but I believe you. And I appreciate the advice." The seriousness of the situation could not be overstated. Ken continued, "It sounds like this will be a rocky road. I'm glad to have you in my corner."

"I'm always here for you. Reach back out early next week and let me know how your calls went. I'll be especially interested in how you felt before, during, and after each call. For now, you need to have a talk with Veronica and practice your new line," Jim said with a sly smile.

"I lost my job!" Ken exclaimed again. He promised to get back with his dad the next week. They finished up their conversation, chatting about family and football.

"I lost my job," Ken said, looking in the rearview mirror at a stop sign. It was somewhat funny when he shouted those words at his dad, but now it felt different. Ken felt sad and pathetic. He'd never been involuntarily unemployed. He looked back into his own eyes and didn't see the spark that was there just a week ago. Ken was injured and still feeling the effects of self-pity. The light changed, and he sped away.

As Ken drove down the road, he took a series of deep breaths. He shook his head as if the demons within would fall out. Ken wasn't happy with his own mental state. Once he was stopped at the next red light, he looked in the mirror again. "I lost my job. I'm unemployed." The words, almost inaudible, barely made it past his lips. Ken's eyes began to well, and his throat choked up. He was hitting an unexpected bottom at an unexpected time.

When the light turned green, Ken pulled into a fast food restaurant parking lot to gain his composure. He slid the shifter into park and unbuckled his belt. Ken flipped down the visor and opened the vanity mirror. His eyes were red and glossy. He took another deep breath.

"I lost my job. I'm unemployed," Ken said a little louder than the last time.

"I lost my job. I'm unemployed," he forced.

"I lost my job. I'm unemployed," he said in a monotone voice. He looked at himself again. Ken saw a man reckoning his life and livelihood. He saw a man at a crossroad, partially defeated and partially enlivened. There was loss, but there was a glint of opportunity. Life wasn't over, only the last chapter had ended on someone else's terms. The lack of control shook Ken to his core.

"I lost my job. I'm unemployed, but it's only temporary," Ken cried. "Where did that come from," he thought. Temporary. It *was* temporary. He wouldn't be unemployed forever. Some weight lifted from Ken's shoulders as he took another deep breath. Yes, this was temporary.

"It's temporary…it's temporary," he repeated. It was time to phone a friend, right there and right then. Ken grabbed his cell phone, pulled up his favorites, and pressed the icon to call Justin, his long-time friend. Justin's infectious positive attitude would surely lift Ken's spirits.

"Hey bud," Justin answered, drawing out the long a sound in hey. "Long time. What's shakin'?" Every time Ken talked to Justin it was like they spoke a few days before. This time it had been a few months.

"Hey, man. I can't lie, a lot's shaking. Most importantly, I'm shaking. I lost my job," Ken answered honestly. "I'm unemployed for the first time in twenty-five years."

"Oh, no. I'm so sorry bud. That stinks. I'm here for you. Are you okay, financially?" Justin's mind moved a thousand miles an hour. He frequently bounced from one idea to another. He and Ken had worked together for a few years at Parkwood. They were a bit of yin and yang, Ken being the calm and collected one while Justin was energetic and spontaneous.

"Yeah, I'm good money-wise for now. I called you because I've never been in this position before and I'm struggling with the reality of it all. Twelve years is a long time to invest only to find yourself on the unemployment line. And, I know you've been there before," Ken said, referring to the time when Justin went through a reduction in force at his stop after Parkwood.

"I could talk all day about that experience. But I wouldn't trade it for the world. The beginning was the toughest, for sure. My head was spinning for a couple weeks until it finally sunk in," Justin remarked.

"How'd you finally break through and accept what happened?" Ken asked.

"It took a lot of self-talk and a lot of sharing my circumstance. Two main ideas carried me through when I was at my low points. First, have you ever heard that you're snared by the words of your mouth?" Justin inquired.

Ken paused, "Yeah, but it's been a long time."

"The words you speak have a powerful impact over what your mind thinks. It's paramount that you speak positive words about yourself. Let's say that you're trying to accept what happened and you keep saying to yourself, 'I got fired.' That's not going to help, even if it's true. You'd have to say, 'I lost my job, and I'm going to find my dream role!' See the difference?"

Ken paused again. Justin really had him thinking. "I do. I also realize that I've given similar advice to people over the years, and now I'm getting it back."

"Yeah bud, *you* gave me this advice years ago," Justin said, laughing at the irony.

"No wonder it sounded familiar!" At this point, both were chuckling.

"Okay," said Justin, "maybe you'll remember this one too. Whatever the mind can conceive and believe, it can achieve."

"Napoleon Hill! Of course. That's one of my favorite quotes," Ken exclaimed.

"It's true bro. You've got to get forward focused and stop dwelling in the past. It's over. On Sunday, my pastor said that your past is a weed, so quit watering it. Ken, put the watering can down!" Justin commanded.

Justin frequently made great points by introducing multiple sources of influence. This tactic ensured his audience grasped his message, which made him an effective public speaker.

"Alright, I'm with you. I needed to hear this today. I get it. The past is the past, and I have to leave it there and move on. I won't let my mind get in the way of my success. If I believe it, I can achieve it. I need to make a list of new goals…"

Justin interrupted, "Heck yeah, you do! You taught me that too. I know that you've been sitting on some personal goals for a while. Time to dust them off and get cracking!" Justin's enthusiasm was contagious. Ken felt himself fill with excitement about setting new goals.

"This is exactly what I needed," Ken admitted.

"I got one more thing for you, and this may be the most important one of all. You have to get plugged into some groups around town. I'm sure there is one for professionals in career transition like you. Plus, you'll want to look for other professional organizations that can help you network. Oh, and don't forget to continue your volunteer work. I know you do a lot with your church and with the homeless shelter, so don't leave them by the wayside. The people you're working side by side with will want to help you. Share your story with them. Networking will lead you to your next gig, take my word," Justin said.

"Okay. I will Google the groups tonight and get out next week to meet some folks," Ken said.

"Hey man, I've got to run. Buzz me back next week and let me know how things are going," Justin concluded.

"Will do," Ken said, "Thanks for talking me through this. I owe you."

"You owe me nothing. Keep up the positive self-talk and get yourself out there networking," Justin said. "Talk later, bro. Bye."

Ken put his phone in the cupholder and looked out the windshield. A smile came over his face. He knew Justin was right about everything, and it was time to accept the present and start working toward a brighter future.

4 – Plugged In

After dinner, Ken Googled career transition groups in his city. He was amazed at the search results; four unique entities topped the list. The first one stood out – The Job Search Network, or JSN for short, with the tagline, "Career transition and business networking group specializing in connecting people to resources."

Ken spent some time reading the various pages on the JSN website and then moved on to some articles. He read testimony after testimony from job seekers that had landed new roles through their association with JSN. The more he read, the more he wanted to see this group in action. This so-called support group got results.

"Hey honey," Ken called to Veronica, as she was walking into the living room from the kitchen. "Would you mind if I went to a job search meeting on Wednesday morning?"

"That's a great idea. What time?" Veronica asked.

"I'll leave around 8:30 and probably get back around lunchtime," Ken said as he scrolled through the JSN page.

"Ok. Sounds like fun," Veronica sneered with a bit of sarcasm in her tone. She knew Ken didn't like to ask for help, and he wasn't fond of networking. He was an introvert in most social situations and didn't go out of his way to meet new people.

"They always say that what doesn't kill us makes us stronger," Ken replied. "Plus, my network is pretty non-existent. I trust Justin, and he whole-heartedly believes that my next opportunity will come from networking. The longer I delay in meeting people, the longer I'll be unemployed."

"I support you 100%! I'm already looking forward to your meeting debrief," Veronica said. Ken frequently gave Veronica play-by-play debriefs of work meetings to get her valuable opinions and insights. This would be no different.

"You always support me. Thank you," Ken said lovingly.

Over the next few days, Ken did some more research on local groups that help professionals in job transition. Just reading about how others were finding jobs helped him cope with his situation and accept the present circumstances.

Wednesday came more quickly than Ken anticipated. When his wake-up alarm sounded, he was slow to emerge from his slumber. Anxious about the unknown trek before him, Ken wanted to go back to bed. "Couldn't the Job Search Network wait for another week?" he thought.

There was no shortage of Wednesdays. But, as he rested there, guilt started to replace the anxiety. With each passing second, he could feel the weight on his mind get heavier. Finally, he flipped off the covers and retreated to the bathroom to begin his morning routine.

A good shave and a shower reminded Ken how he'd spent countless mornings getting ready for work. Today had that work-like feel, and it felt good.

Ken made his way to the closet and assessed his clothing options. "Should I go with a suit or just a dress shirt?" he asked himself.

Veronica walked by and saw him gazing, a bit lost, into the closet. "Don't wear a suit. You haven't worn one in years. Just go with a dress shirt; you'll be more comfortable."

"You know me too well," Ken chuckled. He plucked out one of his favorite shirts and got dressed.

On the way to JSN, Ken daydreamed about what the meeting might look and sound like. He wondered how many people would be there. He wondered if he'd know anyone, if they were nice, if they could really help and if he would fit in. As he got closer, his anxiety grew. He could feel his heart rate was up, and his Fitbit confirmed with a reading of 124bpm.

Ken pulled into the parking lot of the local church that hosted the JSN meetings. The setting seemed perfect and intentional. Here he was at a church, a place founded on hope, to meet with people who've lost their jobs and are in desperate need of hope. His pulse slowed a bit, but he was still nervous.

He grabbed the brass handle of the heavy wooden entry door and pulled it open. No one was there to greet him, but he could hear many voices, some singing, and an organ playing. He saw a sign that read, "JSN meets in the auditorium, directly ahead!" with an arrow pointing straight down the hall.

Ken proceeded through the wide, bright hallway, a muddle of sounds echoing off the slick glazed brick walls and tile floors. He came to wide-open double doors and a sign indicating he was at the auditorium. As he walked through the threshold, a cheery gentleman welcomed him into the room.

"Good morning! My name is Shawn, welcome to JSN!" Shawn held his hand out to shake Ken's.

"Good morning to you," Ken replied as he shook Shawn's hand.

"Is this your first time here at JSN?" Shawn asked. Shawn was dressed in a business suit, complete with tie and wore a nametag indicating he was on the membership team.

"Yes, it is," Ken said.

"Fantastic! Welcome to the group!" Shawn said enthusiastically, grabbing Ken's hand again for a lively handshake. "You've made a great decision in coming here. We're all here to help you find your next career home!" Shawn's excitement was genuine and helped to ease Ken's anxiety. "We'll have to get together sometime soon so that you can tell me your story."

"Ok," Ken murmured, a bit stunned that Shawn was interested in his story. As quickly as that greeting occurred, Shawn was on to welcome the next person coming in the door.

"Hey, over here," a high voice called out. Ken looked and saw a woman sitting at a table looking at him and waving her hand.

"Me?" Ken asked, pointing to himself as he took a few steps in her direction.

"Yes, come on over and let's get you checked in," she said as though he was a lost child on a field trip. "My name's Shelly, and you are?" she said as she stood up.

"I'm Ken. I lost my job, and I found this group online, so I thought I'd come to check it out," Ken admitted.

"Check it out?! There's a limit on checking it out – one per person," Shelly joked. "But seriously, you're in the right place. If you're serious about finding your next career, there's no better group to join. Fill this out with your name, email, and phone number, and I'll get you in the system. Then write some details about yourself for your elevator speech on the second page. All the newbies introduce themselves and pitch their elevator speeches. Just follow the prompts." Ken could tell that Shelly meant business.

"Yes, ma'am," Ken acknowledged. He complied, filled out the requested information, and handed the top sheet back to Shelly.

"Perfect. I've got to check some more folks in, but I'd love to hear your story. Maybe we can chat after the meeting," Shelly said.

"Ok. Only if you tell me your story too," Ken replied. He was surprised he came up with such a quick rebuttal.

"Deal!" Shelly exclaimed.

Ken stepped away from the table and surveyed the room. The auditorium was typical of an old church. A stage set off in the back and was covered with various set decorations from a prior performance. Various religious paintings and sculptures adorned the high walls which were clad with dark wood from the floor to eye-level. A dozen long tables stood in no particular order, each surrounded with eight cushioned chairs. There was a podium at the front of the room and a large screen off to the side.

Several people were scurrying around checking on equipment and handouts. Ken walked over to one of the tables and sat down. Only a third of the chairs were taken, and Ken wondered if the entire room would fill up. He scribbled down some notes for his elevator speech. At next glance, the room was full. He couldn't believe his eyes. Almost one hundred people were hunting for jobs.

Suddenly, the loud roar of conversation quieted. A tall, well-dressed lady approached the podium.

"Good morning! I'm Lynn, and I'm your facilitator this morning. I'm a senior account executive that thrives on personal connections with my customers. I've helped my customers achieve cost savings of up to 50%, and I've been named to the President's Club six times in my career. I've managed accounts from just a few thousand dollars to tens of millions of dollars. I'm looking for a role as an account manager for a large company where I can leverage my relationship building and cost savings skills. Again, I'm Lynn, and I'm a senior account executive." Lynn's flawless elevator speech delivery indicated both her high degree of professionalism and her discipline to nail it down. The bar Ken needed to jump over moved a bit higher.

"I'm excited to be here this morning, and you should be too! This is THE place to be on Wednesday mornings. Let's kick things off with our new members. Would all of the first-timers please come to the front, and bring your elevator speech notes?" Lynn requested.

Ten people, including Ken, slowly got up and made their way to the front of the auditorium. The room layout didn't allow for swift movements from the back to the front, and Ken had to maneuver through a maze of tables and chairs, leaving him last to arrive…right next to Lynn.

Lynn glanced at Ken, smiled, and held out the microphone. Reluctantly, Ken grasped it with a shaking hand. "Uh, I'm Ken, and I'm a project manager. I, uh, worked in the safety industry for the last twelve years. My teams stayed under budget and delivered on time. I'm looking to do project work at another firm," Ken uttered. Suddenly his mind went blank. He was looking at all the faces in the audience and got swept up in the moment. He couldn't figure out how to end his elevator speech. Looking down to his paper, he saw the words, results, and accountability. "And I get results by holding people accountable," he finished. Realizing that sounded harsh, he quickly added, "in a nice way. I'm Ken, and I'm a project manager."

He passed the mic to the next victim, his hand still slightly trembling. The crowd applauded, but Ken didn't hear it. He was embarrassed to deliver such a terrible elevator speech. "What will they think of me?" he thought. Ken could feel the blood rush to his cheeks, and his armpits were drenched. He stared at the floor and wished he could be anywhere but at JSN.

A round of applause woke Ken from his daydream. He put his hands together just in time to catch the end. Ken looked over, expecting to see the young lady next to him pass the microphone, but it was already three people down the line. He took a deep breath and listened to the remaining new members share their elevator speeches. They were just like him, nervous and embarrassed and lacking polished elevator speeches. Comforted, his pulse slowed, and he began to relax.

The group offered a final round of applause and Ken could hear a few people shout out welcomes. He made his way back to his seat, dodging chairs, tables, and legs along the route.

The gentleman sitting next to Ken extended his hand, "Hey, good job! That's the toughest thing you do here, and you only do it once. I'm Bill."

Ken grasped Bill's hand, "I'm Ken."

"We should chat afterward. I've been here a couple months, and I'd love to hear your story," Bill said cheerily. He was a man in his late 50's with thick grey hair and a goatee. Bill wore a nice suit with a custom dress shirt, complete with embroidered initials on the sleeve. Ken assumed Bill was a former top-level executive, and he was eager to hear his story.

"Ok. You know where I'll be sitting," joked Ken, smiling and nodding.

Bill smiled as the two turned their attention back to the front of the auditorium. Lynn continued to facilitate the program, reviewing how JSN worked and encouraging the members to network with each other.

"Everyone here has a story. For those of you who are new, I know I speak for our members when I tell you that we want to hear your stories. There's something therapeutic in sharing how you ended up in career transition. And when you listen to someone else's story, you're paying it forward. Meet up with your fellow members for coffee, and maybe you'll even make some new friends," Lynn concluded. "Now it's time to network. Get up and meet the people around you."

The entire room erupted in applause. Bill touched Ken's shoulder, "So let's hear it. What happened that brought you here?" Bill's deep voice and his calm tone were a pleasant invitation. Ken shared his story, and Bill reciprocated.

"I'm surprised that your story is so similar to mine," Ken said.

"Well, just about every story you'll hear is the same. Some people had plenty of notice, and some people got no notice," Bill revealed as he shifted on his chair. "So, are you looking to continue as a project manager? What businesses are you targeting?"

Ken paused; puzzled. He squinted and rubbed his chin. He hadn't considered any details about his job search. "I guess. I haven't even started looking for a job. I'm just getting started."

"Don't worry. You're plugging in here and beginning to network. That's a huge step. Next, you'll want to get focused on what kind of role you're looking for and which companies you want to work for. This is your chance to find your dream job. You don't want to pass it up," Bill counseled.

Ken's ears perked up when he heard "dream job." Ken needed to know more. "Bill, you mean I should be looking for my dream job?" he asked.

"Yeah, man. This is *your* time. This is *my* time, too!" Bill exclaimed. "I'm chasing more than a job; I'm chasing a new career filled with all the things I never had before. I want mentoring, great compensation, more time off, and great people to work for, along with a mission I believe in. No, I'm not settling for anything less."

"It sounds like you know exactly what you want. How did you figure all that out?" Ken inquired.

Bill reached inside his coat and pulled out a business card. "I tell you what, let me introduce you to a contact of mine who helped me get focused. His name is Tom, and he's a big-time wealth advisor in town. Give him a call and let him know that you know me."

Surprised, Ken asked, "Just like that, he'll meet with me?"

"Yeah. Tom's extremely kind, and he loves helping good people," Bill replied. "I can already tell you're good people."

Ken took a picture of the card with his phone so that he didn't lose the information. Then, he stuck the card in his wallet. "Thank you so much. This is great. I'll call him right away."

"Good. Now, if you don't mind, allow me to share some advice that Shelly shared with me," Bill said as he pointed to where Shelly was standing by the welcome table. Bill leaned in toward Ken, "You've got to plug into as many groups as you can. There's a group that meets on Monday, The Accountability Group, one on Tuesday, Netcasters, and one on Wednesday afternoon, The Family Reunion. Plus, there are professional groups. You're in project management, so you should look into the local chapter of PMI. The more you're plugged in and networking, the better chance you have at meeting someone that will help lead you to your next career. There are some flyers on the back table with the details. Grab them. If you can, try to make it to the meeting this afternoon. It's only a few miles from here."

"Wow! I had no idea there would be so many opportunities to meet people. Will you be at the meeting this afternoon?" Ken asked.

"I sure will. We always agree that 90% of jobs are found through networking, so I'm out and about almost 40 hours a week. It's my full-time job right now," Bill shared as he stood up. "I've got to go meet one of the other new guys. I may know someone that can help him out. Here's my card. Did they tell you to order business cards?" Bill asked.

"Uh, no," Ken replied. "Why do I need business cards?"

"You've got to get some business cards ASAP. It's the best way to share your contact information. There's a print shop JSN uses that's a few blocks away. Head over there now, and they'll help you with design and formatting. And, they usually deliver in a couple days," Bill advised. "Their flyer is on the table. I hope to see you this afternoon. It was great to meet you."

Ken stood, smiled, and shook Bill's hand again. "Sounds good." Ken glanced around the room, and everyone was engaged in conversation. "So, this is networking," he thought. He walked around and introduced himself to a few more people before visiting the table Bill recommended. There were dozens of flyers for groups, classes, chambers of commerce and volunteer opportunities. He took one of each and headed for his car.

5 – Pointed & Purposeful

Ken followed Bill's advice and stopped at the print shop to order business cards. The manager helped Ken create a simple and professional card to be delivered the next business day. Ken was off and running.

During the drive home, Ken replayed that first JSN meeting over and over in his mind. He couldn't believe the number of people going through career transition, and he couldn't believe how nice everyone was to him. "Bill seems like a very sharp gentleman. If he made networking for his next career a full-time job, I should probably start putting in some more hours," Ken thought. "I'll go to the meeting this afternoon and check it out."

With that decision made, Ken's mind moved to the next item on the list: call Tom. This idea caused anxiety. "How am I going to call a guy, a guy I don't know, out of the blue?" he asked himself. "What do I even say?" Ken shook his head in disbelief over the idea of calling a stranger. He brainstormed several opening lines, and none of them sounded good, so he decided to think some more and call Tom after lunch.

Standing in his kitchen, Ken pulled out his cell phone, stared at the screen, and took a deep breath. "Well, what's the worst that could happen? I'll probably get his voicemail anyway," Ken assumed. He pulled out the card Bill gave him and dialed the number.

"Hello?" Tom's voice echoed through the speaker. Ken almost dropped the phone in surprise.

"Hi, my name is Ken. I haven't had the pleasure of meeting you, but Bill Thompson gave me your number and insisted that I call you," Ken admitted. He walked through the kitchen and sat at the dining room table.

"Oh, Bill, what a great guy!" Tom responded enthusiastically. "What did he tell you?"

"He told me that you are very kind and that you might be able to help me with my career transition. Bill said you may be willing to meet with me," Ken said, trying not to sound desperate.

"Ok. I tell you what, I'm driving right now and can't take any notes, so let's do this. I've got three questions I want you to be thinking about, and when we meet, bring in your answers. It will help me help you. And after this call, email me requesting to set a day and time to meet. Do you have a pen?" Tom inquired.

"Yes, sir. I'm ready," Ken said eagerly.

"Question one: what is the ultimate job you want right now? Describe it in detail, including where the office is located, the type of boss you'd have, the compensation you expect and the people you'd work with," Tom paused. "You got that?"

"Yes, sir," Ken replied, scribbling notes as fast as he could.

"Alright. Question two: where do you want to be in five years and then again in fifteen years? That sounds like two questions, but let's agree that it's only one. Describe your job, the job title, and the company you'd be working for. This time, I also want you to describe how this would fulfill you. This assignment is getting tougher, isn't it?" Tom asked with a slight chuckle.

"You haven't scared me away yet," Ken laughed. "Tom, I'm ready for the last question."

"And this is the hardest one. What's keeping you from getting to your five-year and fifteen-year goals? What do you have to learn? What do you have to change? What needs to happen for you to realize your dreams?" Tom's questions were like arrows piercing Ken's heart. He suddenly realized that his goals and dreams had been shelved and he wasn't where he wanted to be. Ken took a moment to gather his thoughts. "Are you still there, Ken?" Tom asked.

"Yes, sir. I'm sorry, Tom, but that one really hit home and got me thinking. I'll take some time to get these answered so that when we sit down, it will be time well spent," Ken answered.

"Good!" Tom exclaimed. "I want you thinking. The more thought you put into this assignment, the better chance we have at helping you, not just in the short term, but long-term. I've got to go, so remember to email me and we'll set a date to get together."

"Ok, I will. Thanks so much for your time. Have a safe drive home, buh-bye," Ken closed.

"Goodbye," Tom said.

Ken pressed the red phone icon to end the call. He immediately grabbed his laptop from the table and logged on to email Tom.

Ken arrived at the afternoon job search meeting a few minutes early. He'd never been to the public library hosting the event, so he took a moment to walk through the stacks. As he emerged from one of the rows, he nearly walked right into a woman coming the opposite way. Ken recognized her immediately.

"Oh, I'm so sorry, I wasn't looking," Ken apologized.

"That's okay," Lynn said.

"I saw you earlier today at the JSN meeting. You did a great job as the facilitator," Ken complimented. "I'm Ken," he said, sticking out his hand.

She smiled, grasped his hand, and said, "I'm Lynn. So, is this your first time here?"

"Yes," Ken replied. They began walking through the library toward the meeting room.

"Great! Two meetings in one day, you're well on your way to finding your next career home. You'll probably notice some familiar faces from this morning. About half the folks from JSN come here too," Lynn explained.

They walked through the doorway to the meeting room. Ken did notice quite a few familiar faces, including Bill and Shelly. The room was bright, and there were more than twenty tables arranged in a large rectangle, leaving the middle open.

"This is a different setup," observed Ken.

"Yes. The way this group works is a little different. We go around the room and describe what we're doing in our search, and then we ask for contacts with target companies. Do you have a list of target companies?" Lynn asked.

"No, I do not. Honestly, I hadn't even thought about it yet," Ken admitted. They walked over to two empty spots and sat down, as the meeting was about to begin.

"When I first lost my job, I didn't have a list either. You'll want to get one together soon. Without a list, it's like driving with nowhere in mind. And that's exactly where you'll end up, nowhere." Lynn jested.

"That makes sense. I will make it a priority," Ken replied.

The facilitator called the meeting to order and began a series of announcements. She reviewed over two dozen upcoming events in the next month. Ken couldn't believe his ears. He scribbled down some notes, barely keeping up.

Then they began to go around the table. Each person delivered a one-minute elevator speech and then described how the job search was progressing. To conclude, each person would name two or three target companies. Amazingly, someone else in the room would offer up a contact with one of the companies. And this happened for every single person. Ken was astonished. A sense of urgency filled him. He fully understood the tasks he needed to complete: nail down a compelling elevator speech, determine what he wanted to do professionally, and then create a target list of companies. Ken wanted that meeting with Tom to happen that same day, but he would have to wait. Plus, he wasn't prepared.

Ken's motivation and urgency stuck with him once he arrived home. He made himself comfortable at his desk in the den and took out his notes from the conversation with Tom. He'd been thinking about the questions all day and was ready to put pen to paper. After about an hour, he had recorded the following:

Ultimate Job:
- Work 10 miles or less from my home
- Have flexible hours so that I can take my daughter to school and attend after-school events
- Smaller company with less than 100 employees
- Same or higher base salary with higher bonus potential
- More vacation; 3 weeks to start
- A great relationship with my boss
- Mentorship
- Company culture that values performance, appreciation, learning, and teamwork

5-Year Goals
- Get promoted from project manager to Director level
    - "Director of Project Management"
- Lead a team of 3 or more project managers
- Earn $100,000
- Career growth opportunity
- Fulfillment would come from financial security, self-actualization and leading teams to success

15-Year Goals
- Get promoted to Vice President of Operations
- Lead a larger team, 20+

- Earn $150,000
- Serve the President or CEO directly
- Fulfillment would come from a sense of achieving the goals and dreams I've had for most of my life

What's holding me back?
- Education – no MBA and no project management certification
- Experience – I've only led small teams
- Mentorship – I've had learned mostly by trial-and-error
- Unclear path – I've never created a career path or goals to work towards to get where I want to go

Ken reread the list. He felt a mixture of shame and hope. "Why did I suffer through jobs that didn't get me to where I wanted to go? Why did I settle for less than I deserved? And when did I stop dreaming?" Ken thought. But he was also excited and hopeful about the prospect of embarking on a new path, one that he wanted to be on.

For the next two days, Ken focused on some household chores that he'd been putting off. He also spent some leisure evening time with Veronica and Abby. It felt good to stray away from the stressors of unemployment and the job hunt.

On Friday afternoon, Ken received an email response from Tom.

> "Ken, could you meet with me on Monday morning at 10am? If so, come to my office – the address is in my email signature.
>
> Tom"

Ken replied immediately to confirm the meeting.

Full of energy, Ken sprang out of bed on Monday morning. He knew a rapid start to the week would build momentum.

Standing at the opening to his closet, Ken surveyed his dress clothes. The meeting with Tom was very important, and he wanted to dress for success. Twenty-five years earlier, Ken's first boss always said that he should dress for the position he aspired to attain. He was right. It was time to step up his game. Ken selected a grey suit from the rack and then a white shirt. He chose a conservative tie to bring the ensemble together. After a quick shoe polish, he was ready to go.

On the drive to Tom's office, Ken wondered how this meeting would play out. Tom was one of the top wealth managers in town, and Ken was honored that such a successful person would meet with him.

Ken pulled into the garage and parked his car in the visitor's section. He took the elevator to the building lobby. It was clad with white and grey marble, sleek and modern. Ken was early, as was his custom, so he walked over to a common space with some overstuffed leather chairs and sat down. He pulled out his portfolio and went back over Tom's questions and his own responses. Satisfied, he observed the comings and goings of the professionals walking through the corridors. Ken would love to work in a building like this, complete with a coffee shop and restaurants. And the location downtown was within walking distance of a few museums and the major stadiums. It was perfect.

At 9:55am, Ken took the elevator up to the 12th floor. He stepped out and followed the sign to suite 1201. The doors to Tom's office, frosted glass with brass handles, appeared very classy. Ken walked in and was immediately greeted by a friendly woman, "Good morning, I'm Lisa. With whom do you have an appointment?"

"Good morning," Ken replied, "My name is Ken, and I have a 10 o'clock appointment with Tom."

"Oh, he's been expecting you. Right this way." Lisa emerged from behind her desk and led Ken down a hallway. The rose-colored marble and light wood accents brought a smile to Ken's face and made him feel welcome. There were fresh cut flowers on two end tables in the waiting area and two more vases on Lisa's desk. The artwork was abstract, bright, and playful. Ken expected a dark motif with images of fox hunts, more like a stereotypical attorney's office, but he was pleased to be mistaken.

They arrived at Tom's office door, and Lisa invited him inside. "Tom is finishing up with a meeting and will be in momentarily. Please make yourself comfortable," Lisa instructed, pointing to the two chairs in the corner of the office.

"Thank you," Ken said as he walked toward the chairs. Before he reached them, he was interrupted.

"Ken! So glad you could make it!" Tom beamed.

Ken spun around to see a smiling, short, grey-haired man in a button-down shirt and jeans. Tom's hand was outstretched, and Ken took a step to meet him and shook his hand. "Tom. It's a pleasure to meet you. Thank you so much for meeting with me," Ken responded.

"No, it's my pleasure. I love meeting with people and helping them in any way I can. Would you like some water?" Tom offered.

"I would love a water," Ken said.

"Have a seat, and I'll grab you a bottle," Tom requested.

Ken took a seat in one of the black leather office chairs at the small oval table. Tom took two bottled waters out of a mini-fridge and brought them to the table, placing one in front of Ken. Without a word, he walked back to his desk and grabbed a notepad and a pen.

"Thanks for the water," Ken said, breaking the awkward silence.

"You're welcome. If you get nothing out of today, at least your thirst will be quenched," Tom joked. They both smiled. Tom walked back over and began, "So, let's start at the beginning. Tell me the short version of how you ended up here." Tom picked up his pen and wrote the time on the notepad, which was already full of notes. Ken wasn't the only one to do his homework.

Ken took a deep breath and started into his story. To respect Tom's time, he shortened it the best he could.

"So, I'll be honest. I really don't know exactly what I want to do or where I want to work. Bill said that you may be able to help me get focused," Ken concluded.

"He's right! That's my specialty. Let's start with what you want to do, and then we can work on where you want to do it. Sound good?" Tom confirmed.

Ken took another deep breath and sat up straight. "Yes. I've been a project manager for the last ten years. I didn't start out that way. I started at Parkwood as a technical writer with a training background. I kinda fell into project management."

"Do you like project management?" Tom inquired.

"I like most parts of project management," Ken said as he shifted in his chair. "I'm pretty good at leading the team and making sure we're on time and under budget. I don't like when we shift priorities and shelve projects. I get frustrated when we throw away quality work. And I'm constantly dealing with unrealistic deadlines. My recent supervisors don't seem to see the reality, and most of them haven't worked in the trenches."

"With the understanding that no job is perfect, what would have to change for you to really love project management?" Tom probed.

"I'd like to have some influence with the leadership team. I want to work with people who can push me but be realistic about deadlines and workloads. And I want mentorship. My last company didn't do much to develop me into a better leader or project manager," Ken admitted.

"I get it. Let's think about this. It sounds like you get frustrated when you can't control outside forces. Is that accurate?" Tom clarified.

"Well, now that you put it that way, yes," Ken agreed.

"If you don't mind, I'd like to give you some honest feedback. You need to let go of those things you can't control. And you need to address the things you can control." Tom's words hit Ken like a whack on the side of the head. Tom continued, "if you want to be a better leader and a better project manager, you have to own it. What are *you* doing to make yourself better?"

Ken paused. He knew Tom's observation was accurate. "Why hadn't anyone else given me this feedback?" Ken thought. "And today it's coming from a stranger, someone with no vested interest in me or my success."

It hit Ken like a ton of bricks – he hadn't taken accountability for his own development. "Tom, you're right. Where's my accountability? It looks like I've been blaming everyone else for my lack of development, but I haven't done anything to develop myself."

"Yes!" Tom exclaimed. "That's what I wanted to hear. We're all responsible for our own paths. When we take accountability for our actions, we can start putting a plan together to reach our goals and dreams. What would you like to do that will address your development?"

"I've always wanted to get certified as a Project Management Professional. Looking back, I never asked my previous employer to help me get there. But I can make that happen while I'm career transitioning," Ken said confidently.

"You're right. In fact, there are programs that help unemployed workers obtain funding for professional certifications. I can help you get that information. For now, I want to move on. Tell me more about your ultimate position," Tom urged.

Glancing at his notes, Ken started, "Well Tom, I want to work close to my home. My last commute was 30 minutes, with no traffic. I frequently spent over an hour on my way home. If my commute were shorter, I'd save a lot of valuable personal time."

"That's good," Tom said as he jotted some notes.

"And I'd like to work for a smaller company…"

Tom interrupted, "Why? What would a smaller company offer you that you couldn't get with a larger operation?"

"I like working with smaller teams. Plus, I want more visibility with upper management. My goal is to be an executive in fifteen years. I think a smaller company can help me develop and give me the exposure that will help me get to my goal," Ken explained.

"Ok. I'm not 100% sure your assessment is accurate. Larger companies can offer small teams and more opportunities. But I'm not here to sway you. I just want to present an objective point of view. If you want to target smaller companies, I can help you," Tom offered.

"Thanks; I'd appreciate the help. I'm also looking for a company that values performance, appreciation, learning, and teamwork. These are my values at work, along with integrity," Ken said.

"How can you test for company culture?" Tom asked.

"I'm not sure. I need some help there," Ken admitted.

"Evaluating company culture is difficult. It starts with the investigation you do online via the company website, publications, and employee reviews. Next, connect and talk to people that work there. Finally, assess each step of the interview process. You'll get a good gauge of how the culture works. Of course, when a company is courting you, it puts its best foot forward; just like you will," Tom explained.

"That's great advice, Tom. Thanks," Ken said as he took notes. They chatted a while longer about Ken's ultimate position, and Tom encouraged him not to settle for less.

"Let's start talking about *your* path to *your* goals," Tom directed.

"I'm hungry, and I want to earn promotions to increasing levels of responsibility. I see myself at the director level in the next five years and then at the executive level in the next fifteen," Ken said, reaching for his water.

"You're smart enough to know that moving up isn't dependent on hard work alone. You have to be in the right place at the right time working for the right people and have the right success factors that fit with management's plan. If you're missing just one of these, you'll be spinning your wheels. Are you with me?" Tom asked, ensuring that Ken understood where he was going.

"Yes, I'm with you. Please continue," Ken urged.

"The right place is the right employer for you, the one that will help fulfill the ultimate position I asked you to define. We've got to find that first. The right time contains two variables. One is your preparedness – are you prepared, or competent, to do the job. The other is the right time for the business. You can't control how the business operates. And there are many external influences that can shape corporate timelines. The most you can do is keep a constant and honest dialogue with management about your goals. Then you have to do your part in being ready for the opportunity when it presents itself," Tom explained. He paused and took a drink of water.

"So, I just mentioned management. You need those people to be the right people. Your relationships with the leaders of your company will determine whether or not you have an opportunity. If you start at a new organization and can't build good relationships with the leaders, you'll never move up. A good relationship is one of mutual respect, transparent communication, and a partnership to create win-win scenarios. Don't get overly concerned about liking someone or forming a personal friendship, those aren't markers of good business relationships. You need leaders who care about your success and development and who give you feedback consistently," Tom said.

Ken was mesmerized by Tom's words, hanging on each lesson being shared. "I'm still with you. This is great stuff," Ken said childishly. The wisdom flowing from Tom resonated with Ken. It was more than he heard from the leadership team at Parkwood in the twelve years he'd been there.

"Finally, you have to have the success factors; that's your track record. You have to perform and deliver excellence consistently. You have to have learned from your mistakes. You have to show you can grow in how you think and interact with people. Getting there is 100% on you. Books, videos, podcasts, webinars, seminars, and other learning events will expose you to a wide array of knowledge, ideas, and new ways of thinking. A formal development plan will go a long way in helping you. This works best if your supervisor or another executive will serve as your mentor. Mentorship will be key to achieving your dreams," Tom instructed.

"You're right, I definitely need a development plan and mentorship. I'm also ready to start educating myself so that I can take ownership of this entire process," Ken said enthusiastically.

"None of this can happen until you land your next job. Let's talk about a plan to make that happen," Tom said. "I've got a lot of questions, are you ready?"

"I'm ready," Ken answered. Tom got up and walked to the large oak credenza behind his desk. He opened one of the bottom cabinet drawers and withdrew a very large sheet of paper. Tom brought it over to the table.

"We're going to do an exercise I call Career Boxing. I'm going to draw some boxes that represent the types of organizations you could work for, the types of work you could do, and additional opportunities that could result in revenue streams. This will help you focus on a specific type of company, perhaps in a specific industry, that you can begin to target. And you'll also discover some additional opportunities undetectable on your current radar. Any questions so far?" Tom asked.

Ken leaned in, his anticipation growing, "None yet."

"Ok." Tom reoriented the paper to landscape and wrote Ken's name at the top, and then he drew ten boxes horizontally across the page.

"As a project manager, you could work for a variety of organizations. Large companies all the way down to non-profits. Before you say no to any of these, let's list them all and talk about the features and benefits or drawbacks," Tom explained.

Ken and Tom discussed the types of organizations in detail. Ken realized that he had a lot of options, not just in the types of organizations, but in what those organizations did. His time in the safety industry was fulfilling because he knew he was helping people stay safe. The projects his team worked on lowered the incidence of injuries and in some cases, saved lives. Ken wanted to continue positively impacting the lives of others.

"In considering these options, let's dig into non-profits, universities and family-owned business," Ken began. "I want to find a place that has a mission I can get behind from day one. If they have a mission I believe in, they should have values that line up with my own."

"Now you've got it, Ken," Tom congratulated. "We talked about making a list of a few specific organizations to target. I think it would be wise to go home and do a lot more research. Look up the leaders at those organizations and read articles about them. Then, you need to bulk up your list. Now, there are only a handful of universities in the area, so that list is finite. In terms of non-profits, there are many, but only a dozen or two can afford paid staff like project managers. They should be easy to spot. Finally, there are thousands of small businesses. Get to the library and partner with a librarian to help do your research. There should be an online database that lists small businesses by industry. Do you have a library card?" Tom asked.

"No, but I'll be at the library on Wednesday and will get one then!" Ken exclaimed. His excitement was building as he saw a plan begin to take shape.

"Great! Let's tie this up. Today we talked a lot about you and your goals. When you have goals, you develop a purpose for your life. From today going forward, the actions you take must be intentional. If they're not, you will not achieve your goal, and you will lose your purpose. Does this make sense?" Tom asked.

"Yes. This makes perfect sense," Ken responded.

"Great. Your first step is getting focused on the list of targets. Send it to me when you're finished, and I'll see if I have any connections that I can help you make. Sound good?" Tom inquired.

"Yes. That sounds great. Thank you so much for your time and patience today. You've really helped me get pointed in the right direction. You also helped me start to discover my purpose. I'm excited about using a focused approach and targeting organizations. I'm sure it will pay big dividends," Ken glowed.

Ken and Tom made some small talk as they concluded their conversation. Ken walked out, confident and hopeful. He had the beginning of a plan, a good plan, and he had the support of a successful and wise man.

Ken received a lot of great advice over the past couple of weeks, but it started to cloud his mind. The many directions and instructions confused him, and he felt paralyzed to take the next step. "When am I going to interview? Where will this all lead me?" he thought. For the rest of Monday, he poured over his notes, looking for a roadmap. But he couldn't identify one. "I sure hope I can get some inspiration and direction at tomorrow's meeting," he wished.

6 – Process-oriented

Tuesday morning rang in, and Ken still didn't have a plan of attack. Frustrated, he got ready, took Abby to school, and drove to the Netcasters group meeting.

Like the other meetings, this one was filled with encouragement, support, and positivity. Coincidentally, that day's speaker, Heather, planned to share some strategies on how to assemble a process to track meetings, interviews, applications, and other essential activities. This was exactly what Ken needed to hear.

"I've been in your shoes before. I was lost. I was worried. I was frustrated. A flood of emotions periodically hijacked me and derailed me from what I was trying to achieve," Heather said as she paced down the center of the auditorium. "When you're working, you have a routine. And you take it for granted. If you're anything like me, you're clamoring to get back to work those last few days of your vacation. You need the structure back in your life. You need to get back on the rails." Ken found himself nodding his head in agreement.

"What are you to do now?" Heather asked rhetorically. "You're wandering around your house in a robe and slippers, haven't shaved for days, and your rump is sore from sitting on the sofa." The crowd howled at the visual. "You know it's true! You're a zombie whose only sense of direction is to the coffee pot and the refrigerator." The audience laughed and clapped in agreement.

"You lack a plan, a process, a habit. I'm going to give you some tips and tricks that will help you get your groove back. In fact, I want that groove to become a bit of a rut – one that you follow each and every weekday during your job hunt. Are you with me?!" Heather asked with authority.

"Yes!" the crowd shouted.

"Great! I'm going to assume you all have quality resumes prepared and sample cover letters that can be tweaked for each prospective employer." Ken's heart sank a bit, realizing he still hadn't put a resume together, much less a cover letter. "If you don't, that's your first step. Meet up with Bob afterward, and he'll help you out," Heather directed. Bob, a grey-haired man with glasses in the back row, waved his hand.

"First, you need one calendar, preferably on your smartphone. All your appointments and interviews should be kept in your calendar. Let me stop there. The most important thing that goes into your calendar is an interview, but the interview cannot be added alone. What else should you add?" Heather asked.

There was an awkward silence. Ken thought about it but was at a loss.

"Preparation and practice," Heather answered. Heads nodded in agreement. "You should spend a minimum of four hours preparing and practicing for each hour of interview time scheduled. Block this time in hour-long increments on the four days leading up to the interview. And book out at least one hour before the interview so that you can get to the location early and review some last-minute notes before showtime," Heather advised. "When booking appointments and interviews, include lots of details like names of contacts, addresses, and directions. What else should go in your calendar?"

"Time blocks," someone called out.

"Right. Time blocks. Now, what would go into these time blocks?" Heather asked.

There was a brief silence. Someone finally spoke, "Things to do, like applying for jobs or research."

"Precisely. All of the things you need to do during your nine-to-five job-hunting workday need to be in your calendar. Only about 10% of your time should go into applying for jobs online, and that includes the research into those companies and the resume and cover letter touchups. Why only 10%? Because only

10% of jobs are attained this way. The other 90% are found through networking. I'd suggest using a couple two-hour blocks each week to do your online work. If you're on unemployment, add an extra 30 minutes to cover your online claim. Everyone still with me?" Heather liked to take the temperature of the room so that no one was left behind.

"All of your group meetings should be on your calendar. And here's a cool tip; schedule a meet-up either before or after the meetings so that you're not driving all over town wasting gas and time. Those are precious commodities that you need to treasure and protect. When I was in career transition, I always had a meeting before or after, and sometimes both. Two-dollar coffees are your best investment right now, I promise. Pop quiz time. What percent of jobs come from networking?" she prodded the audience.

Several voices came together, "90%!"

"Yes!" Heather exclaimed. "Now I want you to add in some learning time. Who here is working on a certification or is taking a class right now?" More than half of the people in the room raised their hands. "If you didn't raise your hand, are you reading a book right now? If yes, raise your hands." Some more hands went up. "Okay, the rest of you need to get with the program. This isn't a time for laziness and wheel spin. Sorry for the tough love, but you need to get to learning. All of you must be learning and growing during your transition. Why wouldn't you take some time to sharpen the saw, to learn some new skills, or to gain that elusive certification you never had time for? Promise me that you'll get enrolled in a course or class by the end of the week. Say it!" Heather commanded.

"We promise!" thundered back. Even Ken chimed in. Heather was right, he needed to get moving. As he told Tom, he'd always thought about earning a project management certification, and this would be a great time.

Heather continued, "There are some fliers on the back table with course and class listings; anything from Six Sigma to SHRM Human Resource certifications to project management certifications. And there are free courses through a variety of online platforms. Spend 10% of your week, four hours, learning. Spread it out between two days or more; you won't want to sit through four straight hours of studying – it will feel too much like school, and you'll lose interest," she advised.

"The rest of your time should be spent finding businesses to target or people to target. If you don't have a list, create one. In fact, you must get comfortable with lists, preferably in a spreadsheet. Spreadsheets allow you to sort and recall data very easily. You can track everything. Is anyone using a spreadsheet right now?" Heather asked.

A couple dozen hands went up. "Why is your spreadsheet better than pen and paper? Please share with the group," Heather encouraged.

A tall, brown-haired woman stood up. "I keep my data on several different tabs within my spreadsheet. And, I separate my communication into a few different groups. I have one for job applications, one for networking meetings, one for professional organization meeting, and one for my outgoing prospecting emails and messages. I record dates, times, places, outcomes, new contacts, and other notes so that I can go back to them. If I did this by hand, it would be messy and all over the place. I can easily sort the sheet to find anything I'm looking for," she said.

Ken was impressed. He was an accomplished spreadsheet user and could create a sheet that kept everything in order. He wondered if this nice woman would share her spreadsheet so he could avoid reinventing the wheel. Ken made a mental note to meet her after the meeting.

"Oh my! You're very organized!" Heather complimented. "You all need what she has. If I were you, I'd go see her after the meeting and beg her to share that resource. The line forms here," Heather said as she motioned with both hands down the center of the auditorium. Ken bit his lip and began to strategize a way to get to her before a mad rush ensued.

"I implore you to get organized. But organization doesn't end once you've built the structure. You must be disciplined and use it every day. No excuses. Remember, this is your job now. You don't want to get a poor review from your supervisor, do you?" Heather paused and glared at the audience. "Well, do you?"

"No," a few people murmured.

"NO!" Heather boomed. "Come on, folks, get with it. You have to own each and every hour in your forty-hour week. No excuses." Heather's intensity was growing with every breath. Ken was feeling the energy and motivation, and he couldn't wait to get started. Creating processes was his specialty, and sticking to them is what made him successful.

"Quick review: you get a digital calendar accessible from your phone, and you put together a spreadsheet to track all your stuff. Are we all on the same page?" she asked. Without waiting for a response, Heather read the room and continued, "so next you have to get organized in your computer. What do you think I mean by that?"

Ken was following much better than before. "Make sure your files and folders are organized and named accurately so that you can access them quickly and without error," he offered with confidence.

"You're exactly right! Every resume you send out should have a unique name. I suggest including your name, the company name, and the year in the filename. You may even add the word resume or cover letter to keep those documents identifiable. When it's time to go to the interview, print out the appropriate files, and carry them with you. This will help you avoid any embarrassing situations and will show a high level of professionalism. I'll never forget showing up for an interview, and the hiring manager had an old resume. The recruiter mistakenly sent over my cv from five years earlier when I applied for a role they posted," Heather shared.

"We're about to wrap up. Lastly, the end of each workday should include a time for reflection and planning. Book out the last thirty minutes to review the day. What were your wins and losses? What would you do differently? What did you learn? You pick the questions to ask yourself and then answer them honestly. I encourage you to write down your responses in a journal. Key in on wins. They're incredibly important right now. With no accolades at work, you're responsible for collecting your own wins and acknowledging them. Share them with friends and family and your new peers here. They'd love to pat you on the back. Then plan out your next day. Review your appointments and time blocks so that you can mentally prepare. You don't want any surprises, and you don't want to blow any of your chances at first impressions." Heather's message was direct and true.

As Heather finished up, Ken typed a plan into his phone calendar for that evening. "Update calendar in Outlook, update the new spreadsheet, create folders, set a recurring 4:30-5pm reminder for review and planning."

After the final applause, Ken sprung up and quickly walked over to the brown-haired women with the spreadsheet. "Hi, I'm Ken," he blurted, about to ask for the spreadsheet. But he remembered his manners and continued, "what's your name?"

"Irma," she answered.

"It's a pleasure to meet you, Irma. Would you be willing to share that spreadsheet file with me?" Ken asked.

"Sure. Do you have a card? I can email it to you," she offered.

"I sure do; hot off the press," Ken joked. Irma smiled. "Thanks so much." Ken and Irma exchanged business cards and then shared their career transition stories.

Before Ken left, he approached Bob, the gentleman that Heather referenced in her presentation. His reputation preceded him, as he'd been likened to a resume whisper. Bob spent over thirty years in workforce development and helped over 10,000 people build resumes.

"Excuse me, Bob? My name is Ken, and I'd like to meet up with you to review my resume," Ken proposed.

"Sure thing. Are you free tomorrow after the JSN meeting?" Bob asked.

"Yes. I don't have plans," Ken admitted.

"You do now. Bring your resume, and we'll meet up in the little study room next door to the meeting room. See you then," Bob stated.

"Awesome! Thank you," Ken replied.

Ken worked that evening on a rough draft of his resume in preparation for his meeting with Bob. He also got his calendar set up, and he made some folders on his laptop. Satisfied, he called it a day around 5:30 and spent the evening enjoying the company of his wife and daughter.

7 – Performance & Pride

The daily morning routine began to feel normal. Ken woke up early each day, took Abby to school, and then went to a scheduled appointment or meeting. The structure suited Ken's personality and his need for order. Plus, it got him out of the house. The more hours he spent at home, the less energized he felt.

Ken loved Wednesday mornings. The JSN group brought him to life. He felt encouraged and supported by each person he met. They exchanged advice, provided sounding boards, and checked in on one another. Though each participant wanted desperately to find work, no competition existed among them. When multiple people were vying for the same role, they genuinely wished the other good luck. Ken enjoyed the relaxed atmosphere, which contrasted the focus and intensity in some of the other groups. Attending all the groups brought a necessary balance to the search process.

After the JSN meeting, Ken caught Bob's attention from across the room. Ken nodded in the general direction of the door, and Bob held up his index finger, indicating he'd be there in a minute.

Ken walked to the adjacent room, saying hello to a few people on the way. He opened the door and flipped the light switch. The spartan beige-colored room, hosted a large rectangular table in the middle, flanked by three chairs on each side. Ken walked to the far side of the table, placed his portfolio down, and slid into a chair. Moments later, Bob arrived.

"So sorry to keep you waiting, Ken," Bob apologized.

"It's no trouble at all," said Ken. "Thanks again for meeting with me to review my resume. I haven't put one of these together in years. It's probably pretty bad."

"First things first," Bob replied. "You've got to keep your head up. Be proud of yourself and your work. Did you do your best?"

Ken paused. Bob's tone was authentic and graceful, something he wasn't quite used to hearing when getting feedback. "Yes, Bob, I did my best," Ken admitted honestly. "And I'm hoping you'll help me make it better."

Bob answered, "Good. Many years ago, I was a scout. Scouting taught me to always do my best, and I've tried to live by that motto. Now, let's see what you've got."

Ken pulled out two copies of his resume and handed one to Bob, keeping the other for himself. "Here it is," Ken offered.

Bob looked over the resume and pulled out his pen. He made a few circles and then began to write some notes in the margins. Ken sat, silent, watching Bob work his magic. Finally, Bob spoke. "Okay, Ken. I'll be honest because that's the only way I know how to be. This thing needs some work." He looked up and peered at Ken through his bifocals. "I feel like I'm reading a job description, and no offense, it's a generic one. You need to wow me with your accomplishments. I could care less about what you were responsible for."

Ken sat up straight, taking Bob's critique seriously. He nodded and said, "Yes, I wasn't sure if listing my wins would be bragging…"

"Bragging!?" Bob interrupted. "You need to brag. How else do you think a hiring manager will know if you're any good? Your entire resume should be a brag sheet. Let me ask you a question; did you ever hire anyone?"

"Yes, I've hired a dozen people or so," Ken responded.

"Did you hire winners or losers?" Bob asked.

"Most of them were winners, I guess," Ken answered.

"Before you met them for the interview, how did you know they were winners?" Bob probed.

Ken took a short breath and thought back to the last time he went through the hiring process. About a year ago he brought on a young woman named Maria. Once he read her resume, he just had to meet her. It finally dawned on him, "Their resumes were full of achievements. I can't believe I forgot that detail."

"Now you and I are getting to the same page. There may be a lot of different formats for resumes, but the one thing that the best resumes have in common is that they're filled with wins. You're a winner. I want every sentence in your resume to scream out that you're a winner because that's what hiring managers are looking for; more winners for their teams," Bob explained.

"Okay, I think I can do that," Ken said a bit meekly.

Bob didn't detect much confidence in Ken's response. From the outside, Ken looked composed and ready to get back to work. Bob had seen this façade before. He'd helped thousands of people improve their resumes after a job loss. Most hadn't rebounded or recovered by the time they sat across from him. Bob needed to instill some more confidence in Ken.

"Ken, I know what you're going through. It happened to me many years ago. I can tell you're not completely over it. Your pride isn't where it needs to be for you to be successful in the job hunt," Bob explained.

"You can tell based on my resume?" Ken asked, not quite following Bob's assessment.

"That, your posture and the tone of your voice. I've collected data from a large sample, and I know when someone isn't running at full confidence capacity," Bob said, smiling back at Ken. "So, I'd like you to indulge me and go through a brief exercise. Would you do that?"

"Yes," exclaimed Ken. He wanted to do any and everything possible to get a job.

"Great! I want you to take the next fifteen minutes listing all of your accomplishments from your last three employers. These are your biggest wins; the moments you're most proud of and the ones where you were recognized. List any awards and honors you received. Record as many details as you can remember. Any questions?" Bob concluded.

"No, sir. I'm ready," Ken replied.

"Then I'll see you in fifteen minutes," Bob said. He glanced at his watch, got up, and walked out the door.

Ken looked at the blank paper in his portfolio. "Time to fill this bad boy up," he joked to himself.

For the next fifteen minutes, Ken wrote down the details of his biggest wins. Numbered 1-12, they spanned the gamut from on-time project delivery to coaching and mentoring new employees. He stalled out and began to rub his temples. Nothing else was coming to him, and the fifteen minutes were up. Ken heard the latch as the doorknob turned.

"Hey Ken, how's it going?" Bob asked as he walked back into the room.

"That was a tougher assignment that I thought it would be," Ken admitted. "I only have twelve written down." Ken's head hung, ashamed that he failed to recount dozens of accomplishments. Had his career boiled down to a measly twelve wins?

"Ken, you did great! This is a solid start!" Bob exclaimed.

"It is?" Ken questioned, astonished at Bob's comment.

"Yes. And we're going to sit here until we have a list of twenty-five. When you have that many, we can create a winning resume." Bob said confidently. "I've got some primers that can help you think back and recall those elusive memories."

Ken and Bob worked for another thirty minutes on the list until they had the twenty-five major wins.

"Our next step will be to pick the top five or six and highlight how those wins will translate to wins for your next employer. We'll put these at the beginning of your resume to generate interest. The first third of your resume is the most important. It's like a hook that gets the hiring manager to read the rest of it." Bob continued, "we've also got to include the metrics. Metrics equal reality. Anyone can claim they have done something, just like anyone can have a theory. But when you include metrics, you go from theory to reality. Numbers paint a picture for the reader, especially if you use dollars and units of time. Those metrics are very relatable. Take this win here; you delivered your project early and kept it under budget. What if you said, saved 10%, or $60,000, and delivered the final product 23 days early, enabling the company to move the product to market three weeks ahead of schedule?"

"Wow! When you put it that way, it really does sound special. And I can visualize the accomplishment. It has some real meat," Ken said.

"We have to do this with all of your wins. Each one must start with a verb followed by a metric. Your homework is to take each of these and do just that. Include accurate metrics. If you only remember percentages, you can roughly calculate the dollars based on your knowledge of the company's financials," Bob instructed.

"Okay. I can do that. When's my due date?" Ken asked.

"How long do you want it to be?" jabbed Bob. "I'm kidding. Friday evening at 5pm. Email me the list. Then I'll help you get the first third of your resume set, and we can add the other wins in the right places. Be sure to list which company and role you were in when these wins occurred."

"Got it!" Ken agreed.

"We're not done yet. Ken, you're a winner. Anyone that can get to twenty-five wins is a big-time winner.

Most of the people in JSN wish they could list out that many major wins. You should be proud of what you've accomplished; no one can take it away from you. I want you to be proud when you're describing these wins. Before you begin, get in the Superman pose for one minute." Bob stood up, put his fists on his hips, puffed out his chest, and gazed into the distance. He looked like Superman posing atop a building after saving the world.

Ken smiled and chuckled. "Bob, I can tell you're serious, but you have to admit it looks funny."

"Who cares? I'd rather look funny and have a job than look cool and be unemployed," Bob retorted, his tone more serious than before. "Just do it. It's proven to build confidence and pride."

"Yes, sir," Ken nodded in compliance. "I understand."

"Confidence and pride are everything when you're out on the job hunt. If you're not confident in your abilities and proud of your accomplishments, you'll blow every interview you get. Some people get wrapped up in humility and worry that they're bragging. Don't get me wrong, there's a way to be confident and proud without being pretentious. You can preserve your humility and still convey the truth about the positive impact of your wins," Bob explained.

Ken hung on every word, and he knew Bob was right. Ken had been the type that avoided glory and recognition. It embarrassed him, so he routinely shifted all the positive focus to his teammates. But Bob insisted that Ken own his wins and showcase them. Though uncomfortable with this idea, he knew the only way to succeed was by getting uncomfortable.

"Once we get this resume finished, would you practice some interviewing techniques with me?" Ken asked.

"Of course, I'd be happy to help with interviewing," Bob glowed. He loved helping people. "Resume first and interview second. We can't be putting the cart before the horse. Any questions before we part?"

"Yes! I almost forgot to mention this. I want to get my Project Management Professional certification. Do you know where I might find a list of nearby classes?" Ken asked.

"In fact, I do," Bob replied. "I'm so happy you asked. Too many of our folks don't take advantage of the free programs that can help them improve their skills or teach them new ones. The local community college runs a course each quarter. If you apply through the state, you'll probably get the tuition costs fully covered. I'm sure I have the flyer in here." Bob thumbed through a stack of papers in his folder. "Here it is. The next PMP course is coming up in a few weeks. Don't waste any time; get down to the state unemployment office and apply for funding."

"That's great. I'll get down there right away," Ken said enthusiastically. "Professional certification has been on my list for too long, and I can't wait to take the course."

"Great. Any other questions coming to mind?" Bob inquired.

"No. I've got my assignments. I'll apply for funding, get registered for the PMP course and I'll produce a top-notch win list," Ken smiled.

Ken worked for the next two days on his list. Anytime he found himself stuck, he stood up and assumed the Superman pose. He couldn't quite understand why or how a simple pose transformed his attitude and improved his confidence. "All that matters is it works," Ken thought.

Google became Ken's go-to search resource. He searched for and found a list of action verbs for resumes online and began rewriting his wins. He also discovered some exceptional resume samples that provided additional inspiration. When he finished, he reordered all the points with the biggest wins at the top. Ken wanted those accomplishments to lead off his resume, as Bob suggested.

After sending the email to Bob, Ken stood up and again assumed the Superman pose. It worked like a charm. Each time he did it, he felt great afterward. Ken thought it would be good to do right before an interview and he couldn't wait to try it out. "Now, how am I going to book an interview?" he pondered.

8 – Prospecting

Ken and Bob met again on Monday afternoon. They collaborated to create a compelling resume that told a fantastic success story. Ken's story. He consistently delivered high-quality work, on time, and under budget. He helped other people succeed and watched them earn well-deserved promotions. Ken's performance enabled his organizations to increase sales and capture market share, all while keeping the product end-users safe.

"Now that we've got your resume finished, what's your next step?" Bob inquired.

Ken shifted in his chair. He knew he needed to get out there and find a job, but the only way he knew how was through job postings. That strategy wouldn't work according to the 90/10 rule he'd heard so much about. "Bob, that's a good question. I do have a target list of companies, about twenty of them. I just don't know where to start. I mean, I can't just send out a bunch of resumes and cover letters blindly, right?" he said.

"Right! That would get you nowhere. I want you to think of your resume as an arrow. Your job is to fire your arrow at the target. What part of the target would you aim at?" Bob asked.

Unsure about this line of questioning, Ken scrunched his eyebrows and sheepishly answered, "the bullseye?"

"Are you asking me or telling me, Ken?" Bob shot back.

"I'm telling you," Ken said.

"Yes! The bullseye! The bullseye is the person that makes the hiring decision, so your job is to get your information to that person. The rings around the bullseye are other influencers. The closer to the bullseye, the more influence and the further from the bullseye, the less influence. How can you find out who the decision-maker is?" Bob asked, forcing Ken to put on his thinking cap.

"That's a good one, Bob. Well, the HR person is probably not the hiring manager, so I guess I'd need some inside knowledge about the company structure and the job openings," Ken responded.

"You're right again. This is where your networking skills will come into play. It's not like this information is on some members-only website. You'll have to get out there and meet people, present your value and ask probing questions. I want you to get in touch with my good friend, Natalie. She's one of the best-connected people in town. Once you tap into her network, you'll be off to the races. Are you ready for your next adventure?" Bob challenged.

"I was born ready!" Ken exclaimed. The thought of meeting someone new with a great network excited him. He couldn't wait to get this ball rolling.

"Alright. I'll email Natalie and you two figure out a good time to get together. Before you meet with her, be sure you have your target list of companies, your resume, a sample cover letter, and your best elevator speech." Bob continued, "I don't send everyone to Natalie, only the best. So be prepared and make me proud."

Ken had only been back home for a few minutes when his phone beeped. He read the following email message from Bob:

> "Natalie,
>
> Good afternoon. I'd like to ask a personal favor. I've been working with a great guy in career transition, and he needs some help connecting with local executives. Ken is a project manager and could really help an organization. He's ready to meet you and take the next steps to find those elusive unposted positions.
>
> I included his email address below.

Thanks! Bob"

Ken smiled. It felt good to have someone believe in him. Just a few minutes later, his phone beeped again. This time, it was Natalie, offering to meet with him the next afternoon. Ken's face lit up. He didn't expect that she'd be so quick to respond.

He immediately emailed Natalie and confirmed the time and location, thanking her in advance for her willingness to meet him.

As always, Ken arrived early. Natalie's office was in a tall concrete and glass building perched on a hill with a great view of the downtown skyline. Ken rode the elevator up to the 9th floor and stepped out into the cream-colored marble annex. A sign for Sunny Day Outsourcing, Natalie's company, directed Ken across the hall.

Ken walked into the office and greeted the young man at the reception desk. He indicated that it would be a few minutes, so Ken made himself comfortable in the waiting area. He opened his portfolio and reviewed his resume.

Several minutes later, a tall short-haired woman greeted Ken, "Good afternoon, I'm Natalie. You must be Ken." Natalie held out her hand.

"Good afternoon to you," Ken said as he stood and shook the friendly hand before him. "Thanks so much for your time today."

"It's my pleasure. If Bob recommends you, you're special. So, this is more of an investment than anything else. I expect you'll pay it forward one day," Natalie said, smiling. "Come on back." She motioned Ken to follow her. Natalie wore a bright blue business suit and an off-white blouse. They turned a corner and walked into a conference room. The windows on the far wall offered a magnificent view of downtown. Ken could imagine how great it would look at sunset and again when the city lights contrasted the night sky. "Please, have a seat," Natalie said as she pointed to a chair.

Ken sat down and opened his portfolio. "This is a beautiful office, and the view is stunning," he complimented.

"Yes, we're blessed. I feel like this view is part of the consolation prize when I'm working with people that are losing their jobs. I really try to pump my clients full of hope and help them start their job search on the right foot," Natalie explained.

"It must be tough sometimes," Ken hinted.

"It's tough all the time. But I feel like this is where I'm supposed to be; helping people at one of the most critical junctures of their lives. I've worked hard to build a great network that can support the people I serve. If they follow my strategies, they find meaningful new careers twice as fast as those who don't. These are the same strategies I'm about to share with you. Are you ready?" Natalie's look intensified, and Ken suddenly felt anxious. He could tell she meant business.

"I'm ready," Ken replied. He grabbed his pen, ready to take notes.

"Let's start with the first thing a recruiter, HR manager or hiring manager will look at: your LinkedIn profile. It must match perfectly with your resume. I connected with you last night because I wanted to review your profile and offer you feedback." Natalie said as she pulled out her phone and punched up her LinkedIn feed. "Go ahead and pull it up," she directed.

Ken pulled up his profile and said, "Ok. I've got it open."

"Starting at the top, we'll need to get you a current headshot. This candid isn't bad, but we want you to stand out, to look like the professional you are. LinkedIn isn't like social media, it's a business platform. You've got to put your best business foot forward. I've got a contact that will take your headshot photo for $20, which is about 75% less than a professional photographer would charge." Ken made a note to get a new headshot.

"And we'll need to touch up your headline, those words under your photo. This isn't a place for a job title or something like, "open to opportunities." You want to grab the attention of the reader, like a good story. You're a project manager, so your headline should highlight the skills that differentiate you from the thousands of other project managers in this town. Does that make sense?" she asked.

"Yes. Would you mind if I brainstormed some ideas and sent them to you for feedback?" Ken asked.

"I'd be delighted to help," Natalie said. "Ok, this isn't a LinkedIn course, but I think you get the idea. Go in and scrub it up and make sure your work history is accurate. Also, add in your volunteer experiences, including any positions you hold or have held. I don't see any in here, but when I talked to Bob this morning, he told me you were active in the community. Employers are looking for well-rounded individuals that will fit in their culture."

Ken nodded in agreement and made some more notes. "No problem. I do have some additional details to add," he commented.

"What about professional designations or certifications?" she asked.

"Actually, I just applied for funding to take the Project Management Professional course to get my PMP certification," Ken replied.

"That's good news. Professional credentials will help you stand out. Be sure to add them to your profile once you've passed the course. Now, before I can get you connected to my network, I need to know that you'll bring them value. Let's hear your elevator speech," Natalie challenged. Ken had been practicing in the mirror, and with Veronica, so he was prepared to hit a home run.

"Hello, my name is Ken, and I'm as reliable as Old Faithful. As a project manager, I've never missed a deadline. My teams work smart and hard, keeping projects under budget. In my last three assignments, we saved over $2 million. On our last project, we finished with zero defects and were able to bring a product to market three weeks early. I create a culture of accountability and collaboration," Ken said proudly.

"That's good! Can I give you some feedback?" Natalie asked.

"Yes, please do," Ken said.

"First, I love the Old Faithful reference. It's memorable and will set you apart. I like you quantified your description with the two million dollars saved. I also like how you referenced your zero-defect rate. That's huge for manufacturers. Now to the end. You kinda left me wanting more. It's great that you create a good culture, but I'm not sure that you can explain how in one more sentence. I think we need to look at your resume and take one of your top wins and put it at the end. The conclusion should set the hook, so to speak." Natalie's delivery was positive and genuine.

Ken felt fortunate to get such honest feedback. "Why didn't I get feedback like this at Parkwood?" he wondered to himself.

"Okay. I'll brush it up and end with a bang," Ken pledged.

"Great! I'm still visualizing Old Faithful. That's such a great reference," Natalie praised. "Now we're ready for the good stuff. Where's your list of target companies?"

Ken pulled out his list of target companies. One by one, Ken read off a name and Natalie would ask specifically why he wanted to work there and what he knew about the company.

He had done his homework and had a couple paragraphs of notes on each organization. Ken knew the industry, the mission, the recent press clippings, the leadership teams, and more. Natalie was impressed with his extensive knowledge.

Out of the almost two dozen organizations, Natalie offered a connection with more than half.

"You came here looking for connections, and now you have," she paused, looking over at Ken's notes, "it looks like fourteen or fifteen. Here's the plan. I'll reach out to these folks over email in the next few days and offer to make an introduction. When they email back, you get to make the next move. Your job will be to follow up with each person and set an appointment for a meeting, a coffee, or a lunch date. It's really that simple."

"Wow! I can't thank you enough," Ken exclaimed.

"The work isn't over. Some of these people are decision makers, and some are not. Some are HR folks, and some may not be relevant to what you're looking to do. They're connections, not magicians. When you meet with each person, do so for the sake of building a relationship. DO NOT go in begging for a job," she pleaded. "All of these people will want to help you, I'm sure of it. But you should want to help them too."

"How could *I* help them?" Ken questioned.

"That's a question only you can answer. But maybe they have problems that you can help solve. You may know someone they need to meet. I make it a point to end every meeting with the phrase, 'what can I do for you?' And I mean it. In this world, it's not about what people can do for you, it's about what you can do for them," Natalie shared. "Are you with me?"

"I'm 100% with you. I feel like I've always had a servant's heart. I love that concluding statement. Do you mind if I borrow it?" Ken asked.

"Please do!" Natalie shouted. "A career transition is a special time. You never know where a connection will lead. I'm sure you've heard of six degrees of separation. It's true. In fact, I know of people who went through over ten connections to find the job of their dreams. You have to keep working it and keep networking and keep asking how you can help. It will all come full circle."

Ken was filled with energy. He loved hearing these words of encouragement and good fortune. "I totally get it. These are great words of advice, and I take them to heart."

"I've got just a few more tips. One; always have a couple copies of your resume with you. You never know when someone will ask for it. Two; always have a digital copy of your resume on your phone, ready to be emailed at a moment's notice. Three; prepare like crazy for your interviews. Practice questions and answers, video your body language, and dress to impress. Four; send a thank you email to every person you meet with and send a handwritten thank you to each person who interviews you. Five; be patient and keep working your process. You won't land your next role overnight. It takes time. In fact, the odds say that you'll face rejection a few times along your journey. Be tough. Unemployment isn't permanent. Stay hopeful and confident. Never stop prospecting and networking." Natalie's wisdom came from deep in the heart. She wanted Ken to succeed, but she knew he needed to hear the truth.

Ken hurriedly wrote down her sage words. They made some small talk about family and concluded the meeting.

9 – Perseverance & Pride

Wednesday morning arrived, which meant Ken was going to the weekly JSN meeting. Even though it had only been a few weeks, Ken enjoyed going to the various networking meetings around town. He was making friends with some of his peers, but more importantly, he was getting better at meeting new people and delivering his elevator speech.

Before each meeting, Ken made a personal goal to meet two new people, deliver his elevator speech, and give each of them a business card. He had succeeded, and his network was growing exponentially. One thing Ken hadn't counted on was the number of people who needed to share their story.

Ken reflected on the beginning of his own journey and estimated that he told his story about twenty times. But many of the people he met were telling their stories fifty to one hundred times. The grief and guilt of the job loss stuck with these people, and it was difficult to shed and move on.

The guest presenter at JSN that day was speaking on that very topic. An older gentleman, who went through career transition four times in the last fifteen years of his working life, delivered an amazing talk titled, *Move It or Lose It*. The speaker practically begged for the attendees to move on from the circumstances surrounding their job losses. If not, they wouldn't go in for their next interviews with clear heads. The lingering negative emotions would creep in and cause them to lose new opportunities. Ken listened intently to every word, contemplating whether he really had moved on.

The presenter learned his lesson the hard way. He sabotaged himself several times until he finally received some feedback from an interviewer. He was embarrassed and ashamed. Not sure exactly where to start, he began telling his story to anyone who would listen. The more he told the story, the more accountable he became for his circumstance. Finally, he came to fully accept both his part and the parts he couldn't control. He had moved on.

By the end of the presentation, Ken knew he reconciled with his loss. There were no more emotions when he told the story. But he wanted to be there for others, to provide a safe place for them to bare their emotions. And he also wanted to help them move forward. Once he started working again, he promised himself that he'd continue to serve the group. First things first, Ken had to get a job.

After the meeting adjourned, Ken went home. He pulled out his notebook and laptop and set up shop at the kitchen table. With the house to himself, he wanted to enjoy the open space and sun-drenched walls. He looked down at his notes from the meeting with Natalie.

"Print out resume copies. That should be easy," he mused. Without hesitation, he punched up his resume on the laptop. After one final look over, he carried the laptop down the hall to his den and plugged it into the printer. "Four copies should do it for now," he thought. Moments later, the printer shot out all four copies on thick bright white resume paper. Ken carefully took them from the tray, gathered his laptop, and walked back to the kitchen. He neatly tucked them into a folder that he carried in his portfolio. One down, three to go.

Ken continued, "email myself a copy of my resume." He drafted a new email to himself with the following subject line: Ken Jaccard's Resume. He attached the file for his resume and hit send. His phone beeped indicating the email had arrived. Ken pulled up his email on his phone, selected the new message, and downloaded the resume to his files. Now he could send it to anyone in a jiffy.

"Prepare for interviews," he read to himself. Ken didn't have any interviews lined up. His head fell into his hands, but then it popped back up. He didn't have time for a pity party, he had work to do to get those interviews, which led him to bullet number four.

"Be patient and keep working on my process," Ken finished. He had created a good process, and he knew he had to keep working it. Being patient might be the toughest part of all. Ken sat, staring out the window. He noticed a bright crimson male cardinal perched on a branch of the birch just a few feet away. "No time for daydreaming now!" he thought.

Ken reopened his email and reviewed the introductions Natalie had made for him. He looked up each person on LinkedIn and sent invitations to connect. The line baited, he could only wait. Once someone responded to either Natalie's email or the connection request, the door would open for him to schedule a meeting.

He didn't have to wait long. That same afternoon, two business leaders accepted Natalie's prompt. Ken felt like a shark with blood in the water. He wanted to meet up as soon as possible. Unfortunately, he'd have to exercise some patience. After some back and forth communication, he scheduled both meetings. Ken booked one meeting for two weeks down the road. The other ended up two weeks after that. "I can't believe I'll have to wait a month. This is going to be tough, but I can do it," he told himself.

Ken's patience would continue to be tested. Most of the contacts Natalie made for Ken responded quickly, but all were very busy or out of town frequently. Ken took what he could get and made each appointment in his calendar, carefully confirming and keeping each one.

Before he knew it, Ken's calendar rapidly filled up. Between the job search groups, volunteer work, and these meetings, not a weekday went by without a few commitments. The volume of activity began to overwhelm Ken, so he improved his initial process to include some extra steps.

First, he created a separate spreadsheet page for contacts, individuals he'd be meeting with that were referred to him by someone else. He listed the first and last name, title, business name, and who introduced them. Then he typed out some notes, such as something he had in common with the person or important facts about the company. This sheet organized all his contacts so he could quickly and easily review it prior to a meeting.

Then Ken color-coded his meetings. Interviews were red to signify urgency. One-on-one meetings were green to signify opportunity. Blue, representing hope, alerted Ken to job search meetings. And he chose yellow to denote volunteering, an homage to the warmth he felt from giving back.

Ken also added an address to every meeting. He intentionally planned meetings in the same vicinities to keep from driving all over town each day. Gas wasn't free, as Heather stressed in her amazing presentation at JSN. Ken also sent meeting invitations to individuals.

This kept both parties accountable for keeping the appointment.

Appointment notes proved to be one of his best enhancements. By typing in who had made the introduction and a couple specifics about the roles he was seeking, Ken extended a great courtesy to his new connection. The individual could arrive mentally prepared and offer quicker and better advice. Plus, this act showcased his professionalism and attention to detail.

Through the next several weeks, Ken met with over fifty individuals. Each one seemed to end the same way; an introduction. Ken felt like he'd called a customer service line that kept passing him from one department to another. He was an actual hot potato. His spirits were on the rocks. And it didn't help that he'd still been applying for jobs online and didn't garner even one screening call.

Feeling a bit desperate, he called Natalie. "I'm not sure what I'm doing wrong. Everyone I've met is highly complimentary of me and my skills, but all the meetings end the same way; a referral to someone else. And it's not like the next meeting is the next day; it's a couple weeks down the road," Ken said with exasperation.

"Ken, relax. There are no shortcuts in this process. Plus, all these people are doing you a favor by meeting with you. They're not going to drop everything on their plates to schedule you in the next day. You're a skipping stone sending out ripples. Those ripples will continue to spread further and further until you finally meet the person that helps you get the job you really want. You don't want to settle, do you?" she asked.

"No. Absolutely not," Ken confirmed. "Is there anything else I should be doing?"

"To be honest, I think you can be more aggressive," Natalie said. Ken shook his head and wondered what he had missed. "I have a new challenge for you. Reach out to business leaders you want to meet and ask them out to coffee; preferably somewhere close to their offices. If they're too busy, ask for a fifteen-minute phone call."

"You mean, reach out blindly?" Ken asked. "Surely, business leaders wouldn't just meet up with someone they don't know for coffee."

"They sure will. Believe it or not, more than half of them will say yes," Natalie proclaimed. "Business leaders are always looking for good people and top talent. So, you want to get faster results? You've got to get in front of more people; fifteen each week. Can your calendar handle my challenge?"

"Wow," Ken exhaled. He already felt like his calendar was busting at the seams. "I'll have to take a hard look at my calendar."

"You do that. If you're not spending forty hours a week on your job search, then you still have room. You may even bump up to forty-five, but no more. You've got to have some life balance. Otherwise, you'll burn out. Shoot me a text after you accept my challenge," Natalie instructed.

"Natalie, you won't need to wait for a text. I accept your challenge. I know my calendar like the back of my hand. There are still some hours in there I can devote to making new connections," Ken admitted. "And I know how to prioritize, which means scheduling over lower priority events like the job search meetings."

"Great! You got this. I believe in you!" Natalie exclaimed. "Keep me posted."

After the call, Ken took out his updated list of target companies and started to research their leadership teams. Between Google and LinkedIn, he was able to find managers and other leaders to contact.

He sat in front of his computer and struggled to find the words for this type of introduction. "How should I start? How should I introduce myself? What should I ask for?" he thought. He brainstormed for nearly an hour, trying to wordsmith a message that was both persuasive and professional. Tired and discouraged, he closed his laptop and retired for the evening.

Ken got up the next morning wondering how he could go from confident to defeated so quickly. He accepted Natalie's challenge whole-heartedly, but less than an hour later, he was ready to throw in the towel. Ken could tell his overall confidence hinged on his progress in finding a job. When he was stalled, it was tough to keep moving forward. Ken was glad that it was Tuesday; he would see his peers at the Netcasters meeting, and he could get their insight.

The meeting was bustling with energy that day. Three people had landed jobs since the last meeting, and each would share their story with the group. Ken sought out his friend Bill and sat next to him.

"Hey, Ken! How's the search going?" Bill asked.

"Same. I still haven't gotten an interview, but I'm meeting with what feels like a million people. I swear I have two or three meetings every day. The good news is that I know all the good coffee spots around town," Ken quipped.

They both laughed as the program started. Garth, a gentleman who'd be in career transition for about six months, was the first person to share his success story. Ken and Garth had seen each other nearly every week since Ken joined the groups.

"Hello, my name is Garth. This is the second time I've been in job transition in the last four years. I used what

I learned last time to hit the ground running. My story is really one of perseverance and networking.

I reached out to an old colleague of mine, and we met for coffee two days after I lost my job. His name is Gary. Gary introduced me to Phil, who I met three weeks later. Phil introduced me to another Phil, who I met with a couple weeks after that. Phil introduced me to Charlie, who introduced me to a second Gary. So yes, that's two Garys and two Phils," Garth joked, pausing and grinning. The crowd laughed with him.

"Gary number two introduced me to Audrey, who introduced me to Isabella. I had lunch with Isabella six weeks ago, or twenty weeks after my initial meeting with Gary. Isabella connected me to Sarah, who introduced me to Jerome, who works for Titan7, the company I am starting with. But Jerome didn't hire me. He introduced me to Leon, but Leon didn't have a place for me on his team, so he introduced me to Mei, my new supervisor. I met with Mei three weeks ago and finally started the interview process. Do you have all that straight?" Garth asked with a smirk.

"If you count them, I met with ten total people over the course of six months, and I'm finally starting with Titan7 in two weeks. The moral of my story is to keep working your process, keep networking, and keep scheduling meetings. I'm sure some of you are frustrated, but you have to keep plugging away. There were times I wanted to give up, but I kept going. I knew it would all work out. Being patient was difficult, but that's also why I kept coming to the meetings each week. Some weeks I missed a couple meetings, but I always found a way to attend one. The fellowship and support I got here kept my internal fire burning. Thanks to everyone for being part of my cheering section, both then and now. If I can do anything for you, please let me know. Thanks again," Garth concluded.

The crowd erupted in applause and then stood for a standing ovation. Ken couldn't believe Garth's story. Ten connections. It took ten connections for Garth to land. Ken suddenly felt guilty for his quick despair. Garth's story was an inspiration. Ken had heard time and again that he'd have to be persistent and patient, that he'd have to persevere and work hard.

Ken left the meeting renewed, confident, and ready to reach out and make as many contacts as it took to land his next role. He no longer cared about rejection or awkward introductions. "Challenge accepted," he thought.

10 – Peer Support

Over the next two weeks, Ken stuck to his process and continued to network. He averaged meeting with fifteen people each week, and he was beginning to enjoy the pace of his new routine. Between coffees and lunches and the weekly meetings, he was as busy as he'd ever been during his transition. Veronica even commented on the fact that he'd rarely been home during traditional business hours. He liked that she noticed he'd been working hard.

It was a Thursday morning, and Ken was preparing to head out for coffee with a local business leader. As he was walking to the door, his phone beeped indicating a new email had arrived. That sound began to affect him like a bell to Pavlov's dogs. Every new email could be that one opportunity he'd been waiting for.

He pulled up the email on his phone. It was from Ginza Aerospace, a company he'd sent a resume to a few weeks earlier. Ken read the email, growing with excitement and anticipation with each word. They wanted to schedule a phone screening with him in the next few days. Ken almost jumped for joy. He immediately replied to the email with his availability.

Ken strolled out the door with a new air of confidence. He was only an email away from securing his first interview. Ken got in the car, turned the key and sat back, happy and somewhat satisfied. He sent a quick text to Veronica to share the good news.

After his morning networking meeting, Ken checked his phone for new messages. The HR director at Ginza Aerospace confirmed Ken's phone screening for the next afternoon.

Rather than preparing for the interview session, Ken spent the rest of the afternoon daydreaming. He tossed around potential job titles and envisioned himself answering business calls. He practiced his voicemail message. He mentally created his new business cards and imagined giving them out to friends and colleagues. Ken was on a high, his mind completely immersed in the fantasy of having a new job.

That evening, he ignored the need to prepare for his phone screening. Instead, he tried to figure out his potential start date. As if he had any idea how long the interview process would last.

Ken's euphoria puzzled Veronica. "Honey, are you ready for your interview?"

"It's just a phone screening. I'll study up a bit tomorrow. I'll be fine," Ken assured her.

"Ok. It seems like you should take this more seriously. You haven't had any interviews, and I know you want to put your best foot forward," she encouraged.

"Can't you let me enjoy this feeling for a little while? I'm finally wanted," Ken said.

"You're wanted here. Every day. By two loving people," Veronica reminded him.

"I know that. I love you both. The problem is, I haven't been wanted professionally. And now someone finally wants me or at least wants to speak with me. I was starting to think no one would ever want me again," he admitted.

"That's just silly," Veronica replied. "Of course someone would want you. It is just a matter of time. You've been putting in a lot of hours networking and following your process. Now you're up to bat, and I want to see you hit a home run!"

"Okay, okay. I promise I'll prepare tomorrow," Ken relented.

But when Friday morning came, Ken didn't focus on Ginza Aerospace or his phone screening. He was distracted by a noon lunch meeting he had with a VP at an engineering firm. Ken felt confident that this meeting would lead to something big, plus the VP was a hiring manager. She told Ken she was looking for someone with his experience and talent. He poured his time into preparing for what he perceived to be the first interview, completely discounting the value in the phone screening with Ginza.

It was almost half past eleven when Ken's phone beeped; another new email had arrived. As soon as Ken saw who the email was from, his heart sank a bit. The email was from the VP. Ken's bad feeling was confirmed. She needed to reschedule their meeting because of a personal emergency, and she wasn't available for two more weeks. Ken couldn't believe it.

Grasping his head, he thought, "Why me?" Disappointment and despair rushed through him. Ken wandered over to his couch and collapsed.

For almost thirty minutes, he cursed his circumstance. He blamed Mike and John from Parkwood. He blamed his old teammates. He doubted all the advice he'd been given about his resume from Bob. He suspected Heather didn't know what she was talking about. He questioned the mission of the career transition groups he'd been attending. He even accused his new peers of Pollyanna-like attitudes. It was everyone else's fault.

The spiral of anger and self-pity finally reached its peak when he blamed Veronica. "If she hadn't forced me to stay at Parkwood when she went back to school six years ago, none of this would have happened," Ken said out loud to an empty house.

Ken was in a very bad place. He had lost all sense of accountability and relapsed into the emotions he'd felt when he first lost his job.

Many people in the groups spoke of the roller coaster of emotions that impact people during their career transition journeys. Ken experienced his share of ups and downs, but this moment felt like freefall. Just this morning, he was flying high, everything seemed to be working in his favor. And now his world was falling apart.

A beep from Ken's phone interrupted his internal wailing. But this was a text. "Who would be texting me right now?" he wondered. Ken instantly expected more bad news.

It was from his daughter, Abby. "I love you dad. Good luck on your interview. You got this! ♥" He stared at the phone, rereading the text again, and then again.

"Someone does believe in me," he thought. "And right now, Abby believes in me more than I believe in myself." Ken realized he needed to get it together. A quick look at his phone screen confirmed that he had only two hours until the phone screening with Ginza.

Try as he might, Ken struggled to focus. He pulled up Google on his phone and found Ginza's homepage. After reading the homepage and company history, he realized that none of the information was sticking. Ken's emotions were still in high gear, and they didn't show any signs of relenting.

He sat back, closed his eyes, and took some deep breaths. Ken had to gain control. He opened his eyes and looked at the screen again. Methodically, he began to reread Ginza's homepage. Suddenly he stopped, got up, and walked to the den. Ken needed to make some notes. He knew he couldn't count on his memory.

For the next hour, Ken read articles and watched videos about Ginza. He looked up employee reviews. He read customer testimonials, both good and bad. Ken took some notes, but he struggled to balance his information intake with comprehension. What was supposed to be a focused study session ended up as nothing but noise.

A few minutes before the call, Ken arranged his notes and resume on his desk. He pulled up Ginza's website on his laptop and strategically placed his mouse for quick access. Ken fetched a glass of water and came back to take a seat. Rattled, he fidgeted with his notes until the phone rang.

From the moment the recruiter asked the first question, Ken felt in over his head.

"Tell me a little about yourself," she said.

"Well, I'm a project manager with about ten years of experience. I like working with people, and I'm a stickler for the details. I've run a lot of projects over the years and managed budgets in the millions of dollars. I'm looking forward to getting back into the workforce and making a difference."

Ken's last sentence echoed through his head. "Did I really say I was looking forward to getting back into the workforce? Oh no!" he thought.

Ken's lack of preparation and concentration were evident in every answer. He couldn't explain why he was interested in Ginza or how he could help them achieve their mission. Ken's answers lacked depth, and he couldn't articulate how he effectively led teams and motivated employees.

After twenty minutes, he could tell the recruiter had lost interest and was ready for the interview to end. When she asked if he had any questions, he chose not to prolong the agony. He simply thanked her for her time and wished her the best in the search.

Ken hung up the phone and shook his head. He blew it.

Defeated, he sat in his chair holding his head. "What am I going to tell Veronica? She'll be so disappointed in me," he thought. "And how can I face Abby? She expected so much from me."

He laced up his boxing gloves and beat himself up a while longer, recollecting each of his inadequate answers. He even forgot to use the Superman pose that Bob had taught him. "What a disaster!" he thought.

Finally, he'd had enough. Ken paced through the hall to the half bath and looked at himself in the mirror. "It's over," he said out loud to his reflection. He continued, "this moment is over. Dad would tell me to shake it off and move on. And that's what I'm going to do. Live and learn. I will NOT make this same mistake again."

Ken longed for the fellowship and support from his job search groups. They could relate to his experience, to the feelings and thoughts weighing on him. But he'd have to wait. The coming Monday marked the beginning of his PMP course. It would be another week until he could feel the safety and security of his comrades at the job search meetings.

By the time Monday morning rolled around, Ken's excitement for the PMP course had overshadowed his interview disappointment. He sent a few text messages to his most trusted peers, reminding them he'd be away from the meetings for the week. They wished him well and were eager to see him the following week. Bill reminded him to continue networking and to set up appointments for future weeks. "Keep the pedal to the metal!" the last text message read.

To Ken's surprise, three of his classmates were regular attendees of the JSN meetings. He quickly bonded with them, and they formed one of the formal groups in the cohort. Throughout the week, they traded stories and advice. They cheered each other on to build their networks, set appointments, and applied for jobs. By Friday's graduation, Ken made three new friends.

Ken walked into The Accountability Group meeting with his head held high, a newly certified Project Management Professional. But his new designation didn't erase the missteps he took in the interview with Ginza. A few of his friends knew about the phone screening and the meeting with the VP. Bill was the first to approach him.

"So, Ken, give me the details. You had that meeting with the VP, right? And, how did that interview go?" Bill asked with a look of hope and anticipation.

Ken glanced down, ashamed. "Hey, Bill. Well, the meeting with the VP got canceled," Ken started.

"Oh, I'm sorry to hear that. I know you were really looking forward to that meeting," Bill commented.

"Yeah. We rescheduled for next week. I'm following up with her today. She had an emergency and ended up out of the office on Friday," Ken explained. "And that was the good news. The bad news is that I totally bombed the phone screening with Ginza."

"What? No way!" Bill exclaimed.

"Yeah. I tell you what, I found out about the canceled lunch date a couple hours before the Ginza screening, and I lost my head. I was frustrated, and then my emotions got the best of me," Ken admitted.

"Man, I'm sorry. I know this was your first bite and you were really excited," Bill said.

"I was, but looking back, I was excited for the wrong reasons. I found myself in a fantasyland," Ken described. "You wouldn't believe all the daydreaming I was doing rather than getting prepared."

"Actually, I've been there. Did you design your business cards and imagine introducing yourself?" Bill asked.

"Uh, yeah," Ken said, slightly confused. "Were you in my head? Or watching me on surveillance video?"

Bill laughed. "No! I did that, and more when I got my first interview. It had been months with no action, and then I couldn't stop dreaming. You would have thought I was a six-year-old waiting for Christmas morning. I even imagined spending the first two paychecks!" Bill said, still chuckling at their sophomoric actions.

"I'm so glad I'm not the only one. Though I didn't spend any imaginary paychecks," Ken said jokingly.

"It all comes down to preparation and practice. I know you've heard it before, but it's true. After laying that egg, I got serious. Prepping for an interview is tough and takes discipline. Did you have a specific strategy in mind?" Bill inquired.

"You know Bill, I don't think I do. I got tons of advice on my resume and networking, but I don't have a guide for interview preparation. What do you do?" Ken asked.

"I have a guide!" Bill said excitedly. "I'll email it to you this afternoon. Just follow the instructions. If you have any questions, let me know."

"Thanks, Bill. I really appreciate you listening to my story and lifting me back up," Ken said.

"That's what friends are for. Plus, we have to stick together if we plan to make it out of here," Bill said, ribbing Ken with his elbow.

Ken shared his experience with a few other friends at the meeting, each of whom empathized with him. He didn't expect that each person would share a story about blowing an interview. James had a horrible wardrobe malfunction and showed up late to an interview. The interviewer asked him politely to leave. Tina totally froze during a panel interview. Karen was on a phone interview when her 4-year old came in the room screaming, and she couldn't get him to stop. Hearing these stories helped Ken digest his own mistake. He learned a valuable lesson he'd never forget.

11 – Prepared & Practice

Later Monday afternoon, Ken opened his email to find the message from Bill. He clicked on the link, opened the attachment, and read the instructions. Bill was right, they were basic and easy to follow. To ensure this valuable data wasn't lost, he printed two copies and saved the document to his laptop.

Bill's checklist started with two simple, yet difficult directives: expand your resume points into stories and write out answers to the most popular interview questions. A note appeared to the side: "Remember that your answers should be concise. Include enough context to paint a picture, explain the problem you encountered, how you solved it, who helped you, and the lesson you learned. Look up the STAR method."

Ken conducted a search for STAR and discovered a proven method to answer interview questions. STAR was an acronym that stood for Situation, Task, Action, and Result. In short, interviewees would follow the STAR method by describing the situations they were in, the tasks at hand, the actions they took, and the results they achieved.

The STAR method proved a revelation. Ken realized that any behavioral question should be answered in this way. He figured he could use STAR to prepare for the tough questions so that his answers would flow succinctly.

At two pages, Ken's resume was filled with solid examples of his performance and team achievements. "Hmm, where to start?" he wondered. "I guess I start at the beginning, with the situations." Ken looked at the first bullet point on his resume and thought about the story behind it.

"The beginning," he said to himself again. "Yes, each story should start at the beginning. A brief background, including how we got there, should create a sufficient introduction to the situation."

Ken started typing, taking frequent breaks to recall the specifics behind each narrative. The more he remembered, the better he started to feel about his past performance. Warm memories of overcoming struggles and achieving wins filled Ken with renewed confidence. He was writing the story of his professional life; a rich true tale of success and determination.

As Ken reached the last bullet point on his resume, he realized his resume was now five pages long. The unabridged account of his victories was impressive.

Rather than getting caught up in the moment, he steadied his focus and finished the document.

After a short break, Ken returned to his laptop full of vigor. The stories really got him excited about his past, but more so about his future. He wanted to lead a new team to new heights and write new success stories for a new company.

Next up were the interview questions. Ken Googled the top twenty most popular interview questions. A multitude of websites presented themselves, so he read through more than a dozen looking for similarities. He cut and pasted questions into a document on his laptop until he had twenty questions.

"I'm not sure this is enough," he thought. "I probably need to have some questions specifically for project managers."

Ken conducted another online search, this time for questions geared toward project managers. Again, a host of sites listed hundreds of questions. He took his time reading through each of the lists and went through the same cut and paste method as before. By the time he was finished, he had fourteen more questions. Now he had to answer them.

Before he started, Ken paused. "How do I know if these answers are right?" he pondered. "I bet Bob would help me. I should reach out to him."

Ken sent an email to Bob requesting another meeting to review the answers to the interview questions.

Satisfied that he would get great feedback, Ken resumed his mission to answer the questions on the screen. One by one, he went through them. Often, he sat back and thought deeply about how best to answer the question. This process took much longer than Ken anticipated. He had holed up in his den after lunch and hadn't been disturbed.

Veronica slowly opened the door to the den and popped her head in, "Hey, are you almost ready for dinner?"

"Oh my! It's already time for dinner?" Ken asked, bewildered that so much time had passed since he started on the questions. "I didn't even hear you come in."

"That's okay. I'm about to start cooking right now, and we'll eat in about half an hour. I'll come get you, so keep working. I love you," Veronica said.

He finished up the questions a few minutes later and emerged from the den, mentally exhausted. Ken underestimated the energy it would take to answer so many questions.

A couple days later, Ken met with Bob and reviewed both the questions and responses. Bob offered excellent feedback, and Ken was able to retool some answers and expand on others. They also reviewed the unabridged resume. Bob was impressed with the stories. He helped Ken streamline the backstories and accentuate the climaxes.

"Ken, how are you going to remember all of this?" Bob inquired. "You won't get to have a cheat sheet when you're sitting face-to-face with someone."

"That's a great question, Bob. My checklist says that I have to practice. So, I plan on practicing the responses at home." Ken paused, sensing that his strategy was elementary. He glanced across the table. Bob's look confirmed his suspicion. "But I probably need to do more than that. What do you have in mind?"

"Looks like I need to work on my poker face," Bob joked. "You need to do some mock interviews. Practicing at home isn't going to get you ready. Do athletes practice at the gym or on the field?"

"On the field," Ken replied.

"Right! Do actors practice in their living rooms?" Bob continued.

"No, they practice on stage. I get it. I need to be in the right environment and have someone interview me. Have any idea who'd want that job?" Ken hinted.

"I'd be happy to interview you. But watch out, I'm tough," Bob said, pumping his fist toward Ken.

Ken smiled. "I'm not afraid of you, but I'm starting to think I should be."

"Before we meet, you'll need to master your responses, but they shouldn't sound canned. Interviewers can tell if you've memorized answers. It's a red flag and can instantly remove you from contention," Bob shared.

"That makes sense. I don't want to sound like a robot," Ken replied.

"I have one last bit of wisdom to share. The candidate experience is anything but a good experience. I'm not trying to scare you, but you need to be prepared for disappointment, frustration, and confusion." Bob continued, "Let me elaborate. First, too many companies post jobs and don't know what they're looking for. They're fishing with bad bait on the off chance they catch something big. You'll recognize these companies when your discussion with them doesn't match up to the job description they posted. This is a major red flag."

"Why would companies waste so much time and energy blindly throwing darts?" Ken questioned.

"The short answer is that this way is easier than investing in a sound and proven process," Bob shared. "Beyond this frustration, you'll also submit a lot of applications without receiving a response in return. HR and recruiting departments are like black holes. Other than an auto-response confirming your application, you probably won't hear from them again unless they want to speak with you. If you haven't heard from them within two weeks, you could try to reapply, but don't get your hopes up. Black holes steal your time and mental energy, so avoid giving too much."

"Wow! How do they get away with being so rude?" Ken wondered.

"There's no one holding these people accountable for communicating with candidates. And some companies tend to think of candidates as commodities, not as humans with feelings and values. Which takes me to my last point. The communication between companies and candidates needs major improvement. Don't be shocked if weeks go by between emails or calls with the recruiter or hiring manager," Bob disclosed.

"Weeks? Come on Bob, wouldn't they be looking to fill their gaps as fast as they can?" Ken inquired.

"You'd think so. I've read many articles that describe the high costs of understaffed teams, but when it comes to the interview process, I think many leaders are anxious to make the wrong decision. Plus, they've got a lot of other important things on their plates and don't make hiring a priority. Because of these factors, and others, you'll play the waiting game. Don't get frustrated," Bob urged.

"Okay. I'm glad you've prepared me for these challenges. If you wouldn't have shared these points with me, I know I would have been banging my head against a wall," Ken said.

"Please don't think that *all* companies or recruiters behave this way. It's just that everyone I've coached came back to me and described these occurrences. This is again why it's so important to network. Your networking will help you bypass these poor experiences," Bob finished.

They made two dates in the upcoming week to conduct mock interviews. When they met, Ken dressed in a suit and showed up early, copies of resumes in hand. They treated it just like a bona fide interview. After each session, Bob provided valuable feedback about the responses, body language, and voice inflection. He also recommended that Ken ask Veronica to video record him on one of their smartphones. This would allow both him and Bob to critique his verbal and non-verbal cues.

Ken loved the coaching and knew he'd grown a lot in just those two meetings. He thanked Bob profusely for his investment.

All of Bob's advice proved valuable during the next few weeks. Ken's applications frequently went into the black hole. At last count, he only received responses from a quarter of the companies to which he had applied. And he participated in several phone screenings, but communication eroded afterward. Ken didn't allow himself to get frustrated; instead, he focused on networking. And it was about to pay off.

12 – Payday

On one Thursday morning each month, Ken volunteered at a food distribution mission. He enjoyed giving back, and this ministry helped feed the neediest people in the area. They distributed over twenty thousand meals each week with the help of hundreds of non-profit organizations.

Ken checked his phone for missed messages as he walked to his car. A new email message awaited with the subject, "Interview Request – Connection from Preston B." Curious, Ken opened the email.

> "Ken,
>
> Good morning. My name is Amir, and your name came up when I was talking with Preston recently. He provided me your CV and said that you'd be someone worth talking to. We're currently looking for a project manager, and you may be the right fit. Please

> reply back to Yana, our Director of HR, to schedule an interview.
>
> I look forward to meeting you. Best of luck.
>
> Sincerely,
>
> Amir
> VP of Public Safety
> Temple Engineering"

Rather than send off an email haphazardly, Ken decided to think about his message on the drive home. Temple Engineering was one of the companies that had been on his target list for a few months. The reply needed to be on point.

Once Ken arrived home, he was ready to make his first impression. A few emails later, the interview was confirmed for Tuesday of the following week. Ken had plenty of time to prepare, and he'd use all of it to his advantage.

He pulled out Bill's interview guidelines and read the following instructions: read the entire company website, learn the mission and vision, read employee reviews, check the Better Business Bureau status, review any relevant articles about the company, and learn about the company's leaders.

Ken began to prepare that same day. He created a document on his laptop with separate pages for each of the points in the interview guidelines.

Over the next few days, Ken went page by page filling them out with details about Temple Engineering.

As he read the company website, he learned that Temple Engineering was a design firm that specialized in large civic buildings like arenas, stadiums, and churches. They had designed the local football stadium and had just secured the rights to design a new soccer stadium. They had also helped with the redesign and preservation of two historic buildings downtown. These were huge projects with major visibility in the community. The prospect of working on such important structures appealed to Ken.

Additional research revealed Temple's mission and values. Temple Engineering was founded by two brothers, former ministers that witnessed the collapse of their home church. Three people lost their lives, and the brothers vowed to protect church occupants from future disasters. Over the years, they expanded operations and came to specialize in structures with capacities over 1,000 people. Their mission was occupant safety through innovative design. Ken felt drawn to Temple because of his extensive work in the safety industry.

Ken read dozens of online employee and customer reviews. He struggled to find one that didn't shower the company and its workers with high praise.

Employees described a culture built on appreciation and recognition. They shared how managers worked alongside them and were transparent about company performance and direction. Customers raved about the attention they received and how each interaction felt like a true partnership. Temple delivered on promises and went out of their way to do the right thing. These attributes solidified Ken's interest in Temple. He was eager to see and hear how the characteristics would manifest themselves during the interview process.

Finally, Ken used Google and LinkedIn to research the company leaders. The CEO was the daughter of one of the founding brothers. She had been leading the company for the last ten years, years that had been the most successful in the firm's history. But the rest of the leaders were not family. In fact, only one was from the area. The CEO had hired great talent from around the country to help keep the firm's eyes open and looking forward.

Temple Engineering had a great history and seemed to be filled with good people. They were known for their community involvement, both philanthropically and with boots on the ground.

Ken concluded that Temple was a strong fit and he continued to prepare for the interview. Over the weekend, he spent a couple more hours reviewing his notes, and he met up with Bill for another mock interview. Ken trusted Bill's opinion, and he wanted feedback from an experienced senior executive.

At The Accountability Group meeting on Monday morning, Ken spoke to all of his friends. They each encouraged him and asked that he text them with the outcome of the interview. Ken never had such a large cheering section of genuine, thoughtful and caring peers. These people truly wanted nothing more than to see him succeed. The positive pressure they exerted strengthened Ken from the inside out.

Ken sprung out of bed at 5am on Tuesday morning. Even though the interview was at 9am, Ken wanted to get a quick jog in and eat a healthy breakfast. By 7:30, he was ready and waiting to take Abby to school.

Veronica met him at the door. "I'm so proud of you. You're 100% prepared, and I know you'll do great! Be sure to text me how it went."

"Will do. Thanks. I love you," Ken said.

"I love you, too," she replied.

Ken made it to the office building at 8:15 and proceeded to the main lobby. It was modern, lined with angular beams of concrete and wood and flanked by a small coffee shop. Ken bought a bottled water and sat in a large armchair in the common area. It reminded him of when he met with Tom. He took out his portfolio and reviewed some interview questions and a few printouts from the Temple website.

At 8:45, he got on the elevator and went up to the 7th floor. The doors opened into a small lobby, covered in pink marble with a long white counter opposite him. A young gentleman was sitting there, and he greeted Ken. "Good morning, sir. You must be Ken. Yana is expecting you. Please have a seat, and I'll let her know you're here," he said politely.

"Thank you," Ken said, as he walked toward a row of chairs.

"Yana will be out in a few minutes," the young man said.

"Great. Thanks again," Ken replied.

Several minutes later, a short, black-haired woman walked toward Ken with her hand extended. "Good morning, Ken. Welcome to Temple Engineering. I'm Yana, the Director of Human Resources."

Ken grasped her warm hand and shook it. "It's a pleasure to meet you. Thank you for meeting with me today," he said. They walked back to Yana's office, and the interview began.

Ken's preparation and practice paid off. An hour later, Yana was so impressed by the detail in his responses and his knowledge of the company that she insisted he meet Amir, the Vice President of Public Safety, while he was there. Yana left the office briefly. When she returned, she asked Ken to follow her down the hall to meet Amir. As soon as Ken turned the corner, he saw Amir's diploma. They both attended the same college.

"What luck!" Ken thought. He now had a second connection to Amir to go with their mutual friend, Preston.

Ken and Amir hit it off immediately. They started their discussion with how they knew Preston and then Ken mentioned their common alma mater. They exchanged college stories and then spoke for another hour about Temple and the position. Before Ken left, they scheduled a follow-up interview for the next afternoon.

As Ken stepped into the elevator, he couldn't believe what just happened. By the time he made it to the car, he couldn't remember the trip from Amir's office to the parking garage. Ken sent a text to Veronica first and then followed up with messages to his friends. Several responses came back before he could start the car. Everyone was happy for Ken.

Over the next two days, Ken met with Amir and two other corporate leaders. By the end of the day on Thursday, he had an offer in hand.

That evening, Ken and Veronica had a long discussion about the job, the benefits, and the potential for domestic and international travel. There were more variables that Ken had anticipated. He'd never been on the road more than a couple times a year, and those were usually for large corporate meetings. But in this role, he'd have to access various venues and projects all around the world. Amir explained that Ken would be on the road 50% of the time.

Ken and Veronica weighed the pros and cons. Their healthy dialogue flushed out all the issues. Even though they felt good about Ken accepting the position, they agreed to sleep on it and discuss it again over breakfast.

The next morning, both Ken and Veronica were on the same page. Ken e-signed the offer and emailed it to Amir. They celebrated with an orange juice toast.

Ken spent the next week connecting with the various people that helped him on his journey. He sent personal thank you cards and met face-to-face with his friends at the various groups. Ken showered them all with warm appreciation and offered to help in any way he could. Not surprisingly, everyone was genuinely happy for him; he could tell in their eyes. And he couldn't wait to show them his happiness when they landed too.

Summary

Each year, thousands of workers are laid off or terminated. It is a difficult, if not traumatic, experience. My recent career transition brought to light new perspectives and changed the way I view employment.

We tend to wrap our identities around our job titles and the work we perform. A job loss destroys that part of our sense of self. For many of us, we're ill-prepared to handle such a loss, often spiraling into a state of self-pity and despair.

Ken's story provides context for people moving through a career transition. I hope that you can follow his journey and create your own path to success as you land a new career.

Pondering

Accepting change, especially the drastic change of a job loss, is extremely difficult. At the time, it's surreal. So, it's important to take enough time to digest what happened – ponder on it. One way is to reflect on the actual moment, the last day, the termination. Next, think back to any possible events that could have led to the termination. This will help you begin to uncover the emotions welling up inside you. You'll likely experience several emotions during this phase. Tune into them and embrace them. Know that your emotional roller coaster is just beginning and expect more ups and downs as you continue the journey.

Present

Once you've tuned into your emotions and accepted your circumstances, you can begin to move into the present. The present is the now, the current reality. Entering the present depends on your level of accountability. You must fully accept your new situation and all your actions that led up to it. For many, this is the most challenging step. All too often, we remain in a state of victimization, blaming everyone but ourselves for our job loss. Frankly, it doesn't matter who's at fault. Carpe diem. Seize not just the day, but take full accountability for where you are and how you got there. Only then will you have a foundation to build toward your next career.

Plugged-In

Getting plugged-in refers to joining a group of like-minded individuals, a support group. There is strength in numbers when it comes to dealing with grief-causing episodes. The fact is, you can't do this alone.

Your new peers and friends will be there to listen and empathize at the beginning, and they'll cheer for you as you progress through the interview process. While your family may be full of strong supporters, there is greater value in the encouragement you receive from acquaintances. Ken was fortunate to find three groups. If there isn't one in your area, start one. A non-profit would gladly help you get started and would help you get the word out.

Pointed & Purposeful

Many people enter career transition with no idea of what they want to do or how to figure out if they can pursue a new line of work. Their goals and dreams were cast aside years ago, and they've lost themselves along the way. Now is the time to reset yourself. To escape this downward spiral, I suggest having a career-pathing session with an objective third party. By evaluating your career choices from a broad perspective, you can begin to talk through each option and narrow your choices. This act helps get you pointed in one direction by drawing out your purpose. Once you have your purpose, you can begin to formulate new goals and dreams. This step is vital because you'll begin looking for potential employers that will allow you to fulfill those goals and dreams.

Process-oriented

Before you can run gangbusters all over town looking for a job, you need to get organized. Remember how Ken created a spreadsheet to document his meetings, job applications, and other details. This step cannot be missed. By starting with a defined process, you'll successfully chart your activities and create a network web. You'll be amazed at how many of your new connections will know each other. The more endorsements you receive through your network, the better chance you'll have to get an interview. Finally, your process will enable you to perform quality follow up with people, thus enhancing your credibility. Stick with the process and commit to filling out your spreadsheet daily.

Performance & Pride

Your story is full of wins. So why do so many resumes leave out the wins and instead list job description responsibilities? Hiring managers and interviewers want to know they're looking at a high-achieving winner. They don't care about the scope of your influence and the mundane tasks you completed or oversaw. Your resume is the one chance you get to list <u>all</u> your amazing accomplishments without sounding full of yourself. Be proud of what you've done and use action verbs to tell the story.

Prospecting

Your next career is more likely to come from a connection than from applying online. Prospecting includes all your networking activities, from booking one-on-one meetings to researching target companies and organizations. You must get out and meet with people who know people. Why? Corporate hiring managers are usually insulated by layers of recruiters, HR professionals, and the dreaded applicant tracking software. This labyrinth is purposefully designed to jettison most applicants and provides a deterrent for those lacking confidence and patience. Bypass this system by getting introductions to the people who actually make the decisions. The more networking meetings you can book, the faster you'll move into a hiring process with a company you want to work for. You'll also uncover positions at companies you'd never considered. With several options, you'll be in the driver's seat when it comes time to accept an offer.

Perseverance & Patience

Landing a new job doesn't happen overnight. Your first face-to-face networking meeting probably won't lead to a job offer. This means you have to get tough. It takes approximately six months to land a new job when in career transition. This means there will be many weeks with no leads, no responses, and no progress. There will also be plenty of applications that go unanswered and plenty of rejection letters. It's easy to take these sour events personally, but you're in good company. From entry-level workers to C-suite executives, everyone goes through this communication misadventure. Expect that this is part of the process. Lean on your peers in the support groups. Engage in uplifting activities such as your favorite hobbies, reading positive books or articles, spending time with loved ones, and enrolling in a self-development course. Be patient, and with time, your diligence will pay off.

Peer Support

All throughout Ken's journey, he continued to attend the support group meetings. The value of peer support is in the camaraderie and safety in numbers. In the beginning, Ken thought he was the only one going through a career transition. Once he attended a group meeting, he realized he wasn't the only one. Relieved, he began to share his experience with others. This helped him to move past his initial emotional responses. When Ken was distraught and frustrated, he felt the comfort of the group. You'll feel the same thing. When you're down, you'll reap the rewards of encouragement by the group. When you're up, you'll spread the joy to others that are feeling down.

Prepared & Practice

For decades, the Boy Scouts used the motto: Be Prepared. Job seekers would be wise to heed these words. You cannot go into any situation during your career transition without being prepared. This includes always having copies of your resume with you, mastering your elevator speech, and carrying business cards everywhere. It also means thoroughly preparing for interviews. For each expected hour of interview time, you should take four hours to prepare. You should even prepare before networking meetings. Know the person's background and know about the company or organization they represent. Your credibility improves when you're well prepared for meetings. And the key to nailing interviews is practicing your answers to the most commonly asked questions. Partner with an expert or business leader to ensure your answers are accurate and succinct.

Best of luck as you continue your journey. Remember, career transition is temporary. Your new career home is closer than you think.

THE END

About the Author

AJ Clinkenbeard spent the last twenty years leading teams to award-winning and record-setting sales performances. He's guided over a half-dozen successful turnaround assignments and has been noted as a client retention expert. AJ currently serves as the Director of Business Development for StandUp Wireless, and he owns a boutique consulting firm, Brightside Advisers, that helps businesses develop aggressive new talent acquisition strategies.

AJ resides in Fort Thomas, Kentucky with his wife, Angela, and daughter, Abby. They own four dogs: Bourbon, Hollywood, Coconut, and Rooney. AJ earned his BSBA at the University of Louisville and his MBA at the University of Florida. In his spare time, AJ volunteers with the Boy Scouts of America and MASTER Provisions.

Read AJ's blog at www.brightsideadvisers.com.

Follow AJ on LinkedIn at
https://www.linkedin.com/in/ajclinkenbeard/

Be on the lookout for upcoming podcasts via his website and social media outlets.

www.ingramcontent.com/pod-product-compliance
Lightning Source LLC
Chambersburg PA
CBHW032022170526
45157CB00002B/810